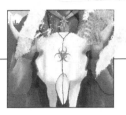

The Militarization
of
Indian Country

Makwa Enewed is a sub-imprint of the American Indian Studies Series, at Michigan State University Press.
Gordon Henry, Series Editor

Makwa Enewed stands dedicated to books that encompass the varied views and perspectives of people working in American Indian communities. In that light, books published under the Makwa Enewed imprint rely less on formal academic critique, argument, methodology, and research conventions and more on experientially grounded views and perspectives on issues, activities and developments in Indian Country.

While work published in Makwa Enewed may resound with certain personal, speculative, conversational, political and/or social concerns of individuals and groups of individual American Indian people, in a larger sense such concerns and their delivery reflects the import, strength, uniqueness, and potential viability of the imprint.

The imprint will gather its strength from the voices of tribal leaders, community activists, and socially engaged Native people. Thus, each publication under the Makwa Enewed imprint will call forth from tribally based people and places, reminding readers of the varied beliefs and pressing interests of American Indian tribal people and communities.

The Militarization
of
Indian Country

WINONA LADUKE
with

SEAN AARON CRUZ

Makwa Enewed
East Lansing

∞ The paper used in this publication meets the minimum requirements of
ANSI/NISO Z39.48-1992 (R 1997) (Permanence of Paper).

Michigan State University Press
East Lansing, Michigan 48823-5245

Printed and bound in the United States of America.

18 17 16 15 14 13 12   1 2 3 4 5 6 7 8 9 10

Library of Congress Cataloging-in-Publication Data

LaDuke, Winona.
   The militarization of Indian country / Winona LaDuke with Sean Aaron Cruz.
      p. cm. — (Makwa Enewed)
   Includes bibliographical references.
   ISBN 978-1-938065-00-2 (pbk. : alk. paper)
   1. Indians of North America—Land tenure. 2. Indians of North America—Government
      relations. 3. Indians of North America—Politics and government. 4. Indigenous peoples—
      Ecology—United States. 5. Military-industrial complex—United States. 6. Defense
      industries—United States. 7. Environmental policy—United States. 8. Environmental
      protection—United States. I. Cruz, Sean Aaron. II. Title.
   E98.L3L345 2012
   970.004''97—dc23
                                                    2012012219

Ebook ISBN 978-1-60917-377-7

Cover art by Bunky Echo-Hawk
Cover and book design by Kevin Brown, Smart Set, Inc., Minneapolis, MN

Michigan State University Press is a member of the Green Press Initiative and is committed to
developing and encouraging ecologically responsible publishing practices. For more information about the Green Press Initiative and the use of recycled paper in book publishing, please
visit www.greenpressinitiative.org.

Visit Michigan State University Press at www.msupress.org

This book is dedicated to three Ogichidaag
who are no longer in this world: Joseph Sanchez and Corbin Harney,
who were both Western Shoshone "downwinders" from the
Nevada Nuclear Test site and my father,
Vincent Eugene LaDuke, a Korean War Resister.

They inspired this book in their lives
and in their passing.

Contents

Vincent LaDuke with daughter Winona

Acknowledgments

This book would not have been possible without a good number of friends and researchers. First, I want to acknowledge my staff and research associates at Honor the Earth: Tom Reed, Nellis Kennedy-Howard, Faye Brown and Luke Warner. Those who rose to the occasion to find obscure facts for us include Andrea Keller, Kai Bosworth, Kelly Morgan, Margaret Campbell and Caitlin Sislin. I also want to thank Frank Buffalo Hyde for his inspirational writing and life, and John Redhouse and Glen Morris for further guiding this writing and research. These individuals and other friends sent in notes to me and helped frame the writing and the stories. I also want to thank the many artists, curators and photographers who have donated their work or helped me locate art: Betty LaDuke, Joe Horse Capture, Sheryl Day, John Fadden, the family of Billy Walkabout, Jim Northrup, Monte Singer, Dick Bancroft, Jack Mallotte and many more. I must thank Mortimer Cushman for a place to write, and his unending kindness. And, my editor and new friend, Sean Aaron Cruz, who saw me through the writer's block and helped illuminate my voice in the face of all of these stories and facts. Finally, I want to issue a special miigwech to those foundations that helped make this project possible: Ben & Jerry's Foundation, Peace Development Fund, Hill Snowdon Foundation and Samuel Rubin Foundation. Thank you so much for your support.

Foreword
Cornel Pewewardy

This book is about love. It's a book about love for the Indigenous warrior, the Ogichidaa, both within oneself and throughout Indigenous history. In many ways this book is ancient because it reflects the most prestigious and influential books of sociopolitical strategies in the modern world, much like *The Art of War* was compiled well over two thousand years ago by a mysterious Chinese warrior-philosopher, Sun Tzu.[1]

The spirit of this book is much like Sun Tzu's classic dictum "To win without fighting is best." This is the foundational warrior strategy and philosophy of the traditional Peace Chiefs of many Plains tribes as well. Like warriors of the past, contemporary warriors are the ones who will be expected to carry out the community's decisions.

Winona LaDuke too, like my own Comanche warrior family, has a rich history of War and Peace Chief warriors. That she began her story in this book at Fort Sill, a US army post near Lawton, Oklahoma, moved me because that is where I was born and raised. In my family, Wild Horse was a war and Peace Chief of the Quahada Comanches during the Southern Plains wars in the 1800s.

Given the historical context of Fort Sill, many early frontier US Army forts were built to incarcerate and control Comanches, Kiowas, Apaches and other tribes. Establishing a similar pattern of building abandoned army forts like Fort Sill into boarding schools for local tribes, the goal of federal and state policy was to fully assimilate Indigenous children into a highly stratified racist American society and to eradicate Indigenous culture. Bureau of Indian Affairs boarding schools were created and other educational policies were adopted as part of this broader assimilationist agenda.

We cannot ignore the negative feelings and treatment of Indigenous Peoples in a racist society. White settler hero worship illustrates a western frontier mentality of "how the west was won." Subsequently, "the only good Indian is a dead Indian" is an American aphorism uttered by General Phillip

Sheridan during the Plains Indian campaigns of the 1860s and at one time this frame of mind was considered a tenable, even popular, solution to the so-called "Indian Problem."

The practice of the Peace Chief is the practice of a Healer. If the warrior is unhappy, the warrior cannot help many people. The work of a contemporary warrior is to take the responsibility to be a self-actualized individual. Becoming more critically conscious of one's tribal identity involves a critical analysis of the social order and a historical understanding of one's position in it. This is a process of realization that entails actively deconstructing socially constructed versions of reality. Remember that power and control are the ability to articulate a concept, idea, or reality (worldview) to another individual or group of people and convince them that this imposed reality is real, is *genuine.* Individuals come to understand reality objectively through our interaction with the external environment which includes other people engaged in their own interactions and reality-forming processes.

It wasn't until later in my life, through a process of shifting my academic discipline in higher education from education to Indigenous Nations studies, that I began to honor the true spirit of the warrior philosopher, of Ogichidaa. Merging critical thinking in everyday life with Indigenous knowledge learned through reading books on critical race theory and through disciplined study has been the union of theory and practice that has driven my academic agenda.

Not only did I find in Indigenous Nations studies a discipline where I could transgress cultural boundaries, it was a paradigm shift for me to move against and beyond boundaries and thus engage my students into critical consciousness.[2]

Winona does not have "historical amnesia." She remembers history through Indigenous eyes. Through her life's work, she honors the grace and patience of our Elders. Potlatch generosity of Indigenous cultures is the solution to the dilemma of modern nation-state corporate greed. Winona understands that embodied relationships must be honored. Therefore, the warrior philosopher model allows key features of historical examples of collapse theory, that of societies facing such crises after having depleted essential resources from capital to waste.

Derived from experiences of Indigenous warriors old and new who have generated an authentic existence out of the mess left by colonial dispossession and disruption, Indigenous pathways can be thought of as a direction of freedom whether we have in mind the struggle of a single person or are conceptualizing an eventual global Indigenous struggle founded on the regeneration of ourselves and our tribal communities.[3]

Her record as a grass-roots, front-line, oppositional, place-based practitioner and visionary distinguishes Winona LaDuke from other activists and environmentalists working across the globe.

For most of her life, Winona studied our absence of focus and grounding of Indigenous ways of knowing. Especially important in her life's work is the examination of the environment that keeps us moving from crisis to crisis with no real introspection. Personal steps toward liberatory practice are a process of decolonization, an inherent tribal right to self-determination.

Much of the process of decolonization is to understand Indigenous reality. It is that reality and its problems that are important to analyze and discuss. Theoretically, moving through the processes of colonization redirects ones consciousness in the direction of liberating colonial thinking and affirming Indigenous praxis, the warrior, the Ogichidaa.

The Militarization of Indian Country reflects a resurgence of the classic warrior perspective in the great spiritual traditions of Indigenous warriors. While *The Art of War* is unmatched in its Taoism principles, the fundamental concepts of this book are the strategies of Indigenous warriorism infused with the key elements of craft wisdom. Therefore, *The Militarization of Indian Country* is not only a book about the philosophical warrior, but it's a book about Winona LaDuke's love for the Warriors of Peace—Indigenous ways of knowing for understanding the roots of racism, violence, conflict, resolution and reconciliation.

My sincere hope is that this book will be read widely, as it certainly deserves to be read, and that the ideas of the warrior philosopher addressed herein will be appropriated by all human beings.

Cornel Pewewardy, D.Ed. (Comanche and Kiowa)
Director and Professor of Indigenous Nations Studies
Portland State University

Preface

I begin my story at Fort Sill, a US Army post near Lawton, Oklahoma. Maybe because it is instilled in my memory as the place where Native men, women and even children were incarcerated—some for as long as 27 years—for the crime of being Apache. Incarcerated after having been starved into submission, forcibly removed from their homelands and brought to this place.

Maybe because Fort Sill is where the Skull and Bones society of Yale is accused of grave robbing, exhuming, stealing and then desecrating the bones of Goyathlay, or *Geronimo*, the great Apache chief.

Or perhaps because today the Comanche people are asking Fort Sill management not to destroy Medicine Bluff, a sacred site of their people. A small request, it would seem, at the only active military installation still remaining from the Indian Wars of the 1800s and at the largest artillery range in the world.

I do not hate the military. I do despise militarization and its impacts on men, women, children, and the land. The chilling facts are that the United States is the largest purveyor of weapons in the world, and that millions of people have no land, food, homes, clean air or water, and often, limbs, because of the military funded by my tax dollars. Countless thousands of square miles of Mother Earth are already contaminated, bombed, poisoned, scorched, gassed, bombarded, rocketed, strafed, torpedoed, defoliated, land-mined, strip-mined, made radioactive and uninhabitable.

I despise militarization because those who are most likely to be impacted or killed by the military are civilian non-combatants. Since the Second World War, more than four fifths of the people killed in war have been civilians. Globally there are some 16 million refugees from war.

I will say as a personal note that I come from a family of people who love peace. My father, Vincent Eugene LaDuke (who was known most of his life as Sun Bear), was a conscientious objector to serving in the Korean War, and he spent eleven months in prison for his beliefs. My mother Betty LaDuke and stepfather Peter Westigard took me to many anti-Vietnam War demonstrations as a young child in a conservative county.

I have opposed every war since my childhood, and will likely oppose the next war before it even begins. I believe, however, that there can be a righteous reason to fight, and I respect those who have served their nation, their People. I believe that veterans should be treated with honor and dignity, despite the military policies of this country.

I decided to write this book because I am awed by the impact of the military on the world and on Native America. It is pervasive. Native people have seen our communities, lands and life ways destroyed by the military. Since the first European colonizers arrived, the US military has been a blunt instrument of genocide, carrying out policies of removal and extermination against Native Peoples. Following the Indian Wars, we experienced the forced assimilation of boarding schools, which were founded by an army colonel, Richard Pratt, and which left a history of transformative loss of language and culture.

The modern US military has taken our lands for bombing exercises and military bases, and for the experimentation and storage of the deadliest chemical agents and toxins known to mankind. Today, the military continues to bomb Native Hawaiian lands, from Makua to the Big Island, destroying life.

The military has named us and claimed us. Many of our tribal communities are named after the forts that once held our people captive, and in today's military nomenclature Osama bin Laden, the recently killed leader of al Qaeda, was also known as "Geronimo EKIA" (Enemy Killed in Action).

Harlan Geronimo, an army veteran who served two tours in Vietnam and is the great grandson of Apache Chief Geronimo, asked for a formal apology and called the Pentagon's decision to use the code name Geronimo in the raid that ended with al Qaeda leader Osama bin Laden's death, a "grievous insult." He was joined by most major Native American organizations in calling for a retraction and apology. The Onondaga nation stated, "This continues to personify the original peoples of North America as enemies and savages. . . . The US military leadership should have known better."

The analogy from a military perspective is interesting. At the time of the hunting down of Geronimo, over 5,500 military personnel were engaged in a 13-year pursuit of the Apache Chief. Geronimo traveled with his community, including 35 men and 108 women and children, who in the end surrendered in exhaustion and were met with promises that were never fulfilled. It was one of the most expensive and shameful of the Indian Wars.

It is a hundred years later and a similarly exorbitant amount of both time and money has been spent finding Osama bin Laden. The toll for hunting the al Qaeda leader and his posse, along with the wars associated with it, is over $3 trillion. That is probably where the analogy ends. The reality is that Geronimo was a true patriot, his battles were in defense of his land and he was a hero. The coupling of his name with the most vilified enemy of America in this millennium is dangerous ground.

The military, it seems, is comfortable with this ground. Indeed, Native nomenclature in the US military is widespread. From Kiowa, Apache Longbow and Black Hawk helicopters to Tomahawk missiles, the machinery of war has many Native names. (The Huey helicopter Bell UH-1 is the Iroquois, and the Sikorsky helicopters are also known as Chickasaw, Choctaw and Mohave helicopters.)

As the Seventh Cavalry invaded Iraq in 2003 in the "Shock and Awe" campaign that opened the war, one could not help note that this was the name of the cavalry division that had murdered 300 men, women and children at Wounded Knee.

Yet, despite our history and the present appropriation of our lands and culture by the military, we have the highest rate of military enlistment of any ethnic group in the United States. We also have the largest number of living veterans out of any community in the country. We have borne a huge burden of post traumatic stress disorder among our veterans, and continue to feel this pain today, compounded by our own unresolved historic grief stemming from colonization.

In this book, I consider the scope of our historic and present relationship with the military and discuss economic, ecological and psychological impacts. I then examine the potential for a major transformation from the US military economy that today controls much of Indian Country to a new community-centered model that values our Native cultures and traditions and honors our Mother Earth.

The book is divided into four sections:

Chapter I, "The Military and the People," contains a brief history of the military and Native people, a set of profiles of some well-known and not so well-known veterans and a discussion of some of the impacts of Post Traumatic Stress Disorder on our nations.

Chapter II, "The Military and the Economy," reviews the broad economics of war and then offers a socio-economic case study of the Navajo Nation. This chapter also discusses tribal military contractors, like Blackwater.

Chapter III, "The Military and the Land," discusses historic and current military land seizures from Native communities and the environmental impact of the military in Native America. This section also broaches the history of why so many reservations are called Fort.

Chapter IV, "The Military and the Future," discusses some present positive endeavors of the military, their possible implications for the Native and broader community, and how we can proceed to create a more peaceful world for coming generations.

I hope you find the book's contents informative and, in the end, I hope that some readers are encouraged to critically examine Native peoples' relationship with the military, and start the work of transforming it.

Miigwech,
Winona LaDuke
Veteran's Day, 2012

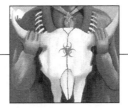

The Militarization
of
Indian Country

My Grandfather is a veteran.
My Father is a veteran.
I was born without my right arm below the elbow.
I was born without my right leg above the knee.

As a tail gunner during the Korean War, my grandfather was shot
down and spent some time missing in action. During his second
tour in Vietnam, my father survived a grenade blast. Before high
school I made an appointment with a Marine recruiter. He told
me that currently the Marine Corps doesn't accept people with
disabilities. They just create them.

I believe the blood remembers.
I believe in defending your nation.
Blood taught me that.

Agent Orange took my right side.
Am I a veteran?
I bare the wounds of proximity.

— Poetry and painting by Frank Buffalo Hyde (Onondaga/Nez Perce/Assiniboine),
       excerpted from an exhibit at the Institute of American Indian Arts, 2007

I.

The Military and the People

OGICHIDAA

Ogichidaa is an Ojibwe word that loosely translates as 'warrior,' but the essence of the word is much deeper and more nuanced than the English. The word is perhaps better translated in the plural as Ogichidaag, which means 'those who defend the people.' Ogichidaa or Akicita is also a word shared between the Anishinaabeg and the Lakota, our "most honored enemies."

The great Lakota Chief and Holy Man Sitting Bull described the meaning of a warrior by pointing to the inherent responsibilities such a position held:

> For us, warriors are not what you think of as warriors. The warrior is not someone who fights, because no one has the right to take another's life. The warrior, for us, is one who sacrifices himself for the good of others. His task is to take care of the elderly, the defenseless, those who cannot provide for themselves and above all, the children, the future of humanity.

Sitting Bull's definition stands in stark contrast to the stereotypes of Indian warriors as bloodthirsty killers, so prominent in American mythology. That is not to say that tribes did not engage in warfare. There are critical differences, however, between a war fought to defend the people and the land, and a war fought to create or sustain an empire, to impose colonial rule on an unwilling population. That is part of the ironic dichotomy in which we as Indigenous peoples find ourselves today.

There is also a critical difference between warfare designed to kill en masse, and warfare designed to keep enemies at bay, as was the ancient custom of tribes. The greatest honor a warrior could achieve was to "count coup" on an enemy—touching his enemy without inflicting any bodily harm. Such an act was a demonstration of bravery and skill as opposed to the demonstrations of immense force that are intrinsic to America's military prowess.

The warriors of centuries past defended our peoples from other tribes and from the European colonizers. Our warriors worked in consultation with our spiritual leaders, Clan Mothers sat in council to seek guidance in order to ensure engaging in warfare was essential to our survival.

Many of our Native communities have instructions on how to live a life of peace. The Haudenosaune Great Law of Peace is one of the most notable examples of how our nations organized our societies to ensure peace was possible. The Haudenosaune tell of The Peacemaker, a messenger who came to the people and delivered a set of principles, or laws, for them to follow:

> The Peacemaker came to the people with a message that human beings should cease abusing one another. He stated that humans are capable of reason, that through the power of reason all men desire peace, and that it is necessary that people organize to ensure that peace will be possible among the people who walk about on the Earth. That was the original word about laws—laws were originally made to prevent the abuse of humans by other humans.[4]

These lessons should not be forgotten.

The Peacemaker by John Fadden

NATIVE MILITARY SOCIETIES

Since time immemorial and to the present day, Indigenous peoples have created and maintained military or warrior societies to protect our land, people, traditions and ways of life. These responsibilities were vital to the success and the survival of the tribe or nation and thus warrior society members were highly regarded, esteemed and often attained heroic status.

Membership in these societies was traditionally voluntary, and admission was usually earned through some accomplishment resulting in an invitation from existing members. With the acceptance of a member into the society, songs, dances and traditional knowledge and responsibilities were passed on from elders in the society to the new initiate.

Some of the better-known traditional military societies include the Cheyenne Fox Warriors or Kit Fox Society, and the Lakota Dog Warriors or Dog Soldiers, as they were more commonly known.

Tribes often had multiple warrior societies, each with their unique traditions, songs and ceremonies. The Mandan and Hidatsa were known to have ten military societies, the Cheyenne and Kiowa had six societies and members of the Blackfoot Confederacy had seven military societies.[5]

Many tribal military societies keep memories alive and honor recent accomplishments through ceremonies and public events. For example, The *Ton Ken Ge*, or Black Leggings Society, of the Kiowa honor historic and recent military deeds each October in Indian City, Oklahoma. They are represented at many important gatherings in the region, where they erect their Battle Tipi.

The tipi, it is said, originates from the Kiowa Principal Chief Dohosan and is painted on one side in black and yellow horizontal stripes that symbolize battles or achievements, mostly arising from their defense of their people against attacks from the US Army. The other side depicts several historic events, beginning with the 1864 battle with Kit Carson, and subsequent scenes from other US military wars. Among the battles recorded are scenes from World Wars I and II, the Korean conflict and the Vietnam War. Recent additions to the Kiowa Battle Tipi reflect the wars in Iraq and Afghanistan and the names of fallen Kiowa soldiers.

Ledger art courtesy Joe Horse Capture. Ledger art is a genre that resulted from the destruction of buffalo herds and other wildlife by Euro-Americans as the US Army forced Plains tribes onto reservations and once-plentiful animal hides became scarce. Native artists turned to paper, which was often taken from ledgers and other discarded materials.

Native American military or warrior societies have taken prominent leadership roles in the past three decades in many conflicts over Native lands and the rights of Indigenous people.

Perhaps the most widely known modern conflict was the defense of Wounded Knee on the Pine Ridge Reservation in 1973. Lakota elders and families, along with Native men and women from around the country, occupied the hamlet of Wounded Knee for 71 days to protest corruption and violence by the tribal government, ongoing poverty and the violation of treaty rights.

The band of Native occupants of the hamlet were surrounded by US military forces and two men, Buddy Lamont and Frank Clearwater, were killed by US snipers. Many of the American Indian Movement's (AIM) members were Vietnam veterans who had recently returned from war to find the army they had fought with against the Indigenous people of Vietnam turned against their brothers and sisters at home.[6]

The Oka, Ganienkah and Gustaffson Lake struggles in Canada were also undertaken by warrior societies of the Mohawk and other Indigenous peoples. As Al Carroll notes in his book, *Medicine Bags and Dog Tags*, "Rotiskenrakete (literally, 'men who carry the burden of peace') or the Mohawk Warrior Society formed on the reservations in New York State and in reserves in Quebec in 1974, seizing an island between Canada and the US and declaring an independent nation named Ganankieh."[7]

Other confrontations involving warrior societies include the Menominee Warriors Society and their takeover of the former Alexian Brothers Abbey in 1975 to protest the US policy of termination. The society demanded that the property be returned to its original owners and then turned it into a drug and alcohol rehabilitation facility.

In 1975, the Navajo Warrior Society took over the Fairchild Electronics Plant—a military subcontractor—"in response to complaints about low pay, sexual harassment, and the Maine-based company's refusal to promote Navajos into the higher-paying management positions."[8]

Dick LaGarde was a long-term member of the American Indian Movement. This photo was taken at the AIM occupation of the Bureau of Indian Affairs in 1972. Photo courtesy Dick LaGarde

The Manitoba Warrior Society is the largest warriors' society in Canada. "In 1995, members occupied Ts'Peten, or Lake Gustafsen, a sacred Sun Dance site barred to Natives. The Canadian government responded with a siege nearly as violent as the Wounded Knee II standoff, with over 77,000 rounds fired by the Royal Canadian Mounted Police followed by the longest trial in Canadian history."[9] Other confrontations of note include the Oka Standoff in Canada, where one-fourth of the entire Canadian Army was called out in response to the protests of Mohawk people in 1991.

The spirit of the Ogichidaag remains strong and essential to our communities whether the Ogichidaag are standing against treaty rights abuses, the illegal seizure of our land or unsound development projects. Our communities honor that spirit and practice because our continued survival, in part, relies upon those who will defend our people, in court, in protests and in ceremony.

THE US ARMY AND THE MASSACRE AT WOUNDED KNEE

On December 29, 1890, the US Seventh Cavalry surrounded and indiscriminately slaughtered as many as 300 mostly unarmed and defenseless Lakota men, women and children in the snow and ice at Wounded Knee.

Eighteen Congressional Medals of Honor were awarded to soldiers who committed the atrocities, and none have been stripped. Nor has there been an apology. In total, the US Army awarded an astonishing 425 Congressional Medals of Honor for killing Indians. The citations do not specify whether the Indians killed were men, women or children as all were eligible for brutal treatment and summary execution.[10]

NATIVE PARTICIPATION IN AND OPPOSITION TO WAR

Throughout recent history, Native peoples have served in the US military in extraordinarily large numbers:

• Twenty thousand Natives served in the Civil War for both flags, Union and Confederacy. In fact, Ulysses Grant's personal secretary, Ely Parker, was one of the most prominent Native soldiers of the war.[11]

• It is estimated that more than 12,000 American Indians served in the United States military in World War I.[12]

• More than 44,000 American Indians, out of a total Native American population of less than 350,000, served with distinction between 1941 and 1945 in both the European and Pacific theaters of World War II.[13]

• During World War II, Native American men and women on the home front also showed an intense desire to serve their country and were an integral part of the war effort. More than 40,000 Indian people left their reservations to work in ordnance depots, factories and other war industries. American Indians also invested more than $50 million in war bonds, and contributed generously to the Red Cross and the Army and Navy Relief societies.[14]

• It is estimated that there were 42,000 Vietnam-era Native American veterans.[15]

At the beginning of the twenty-first century, there are between 160,000 and 190,000 Native American military veterans, about 10 percent of all living Native Americans. This is a proportion triple to that of the non-Indian population. An estimated 22 percent of Native Americans 18 or older are veterans.[16]

Today, Native peoples have the highest rates of enlistment of any ethnic group in the United States. In some Native communities, in a single graduating class over half of the graduates will be military-bound. Many youth, both reservation-based and urban, see no options outside the military to secure an economically stable future.

How did things change? How did we move from being the target of the US military to being the US military itself? That question has to do with the larger forces of American society—economic deprivation, domination and racism—all of which have figured into the high levels of Native induction into the military.

Military indoctrination has long been considered to be an effective method for transforming Native America, as a way to "save the man and kill the Indian," and in many ways it has succeeded. The military boarding school regimes under the leadership of Colonel Pratt and others transformed many of our people from Indigenous Ogichidaag to individuals willing to partici- pate in wars of empire, fought to enforce a colonial mandate on unwilling populations, much like the history of the Indian Wars the US military fought across this continent. The following statement by Tony Blackfeather drives home the similar nature of the Iraq War to those fought against Native America:

> If America, or the world for that matter, wants to understand the mindset behind the war, it's simple. Ask an Indian. The current invasion . . . is the latest chapter in the American colonial pro- cess. . . . We see the same history unfolding that our people have [experienced] and continue to experience. Our genetic memo- ries recall the massacres in our own country. . . . This is the same history. . . . It is a mass murder for oil and resources—the same thing they did to us—the same people are in Iraq that killed my Lakota people and stole our Lakota land. . . . We are not involved in this so-called war. We cannot condone the use of what are our resources to support the invasion of Iraq. . . . The US is going to put the Iraqi people under the same reservation and trust system they have used against our people. . . . The appointment of 23 American 'ministers' . . . sounds very similar to the Indian agents installed on reservations. The Lakota nation stands with the UN member states . . . condemning the invasion of Iraq, calling for a ceasefire and a withdrawal of US and British armed forces. The Teton Sioux Nation. . . . Pray for the peoples and nations . . . expe- riencing the weight of American imperialism.[17]

Many Native communities have not joined in war efforts for a variety of reasons, among them the history of the broken and hostile relationships between the US military and Native people, spiritual teachings and the lack of recognition of Native rights. Chief of the Fairford, Little Saskatchewan and Lake St. Martin Bands of Canada resisted enlistment for his people, stating that, "We have no full rights of citizenship. We have no rights to vote. Nor have we our Franchise. Therefore we object to the Registration of our Race."[18]

In the United States, most Indigenous people did not have citizenship status until after World War I. The 1924 Indian Citizenship Act did not include Native Americans born before the effective date of the act or born outside of the United States. US citizenship was forced—or bestowed upon—Native people, depending on how you look at it, by a piecemeal series of legislative acts and court cases in 1919, 1924, 1940, 1948 and into the 1950s, when the last holdout states finally allowed their Native American citizens the right to vote.

> With Natives now legal citizens, the main legal basis that tribal leaders had used to argue against the draft (and military service) vanished. . . . Citizenship acts, however, did not provide for legal rights, or settle land claims, and did nothing to protect voting rights. Eleven states specifically barred Natives from voting until the 1950s, making it a bit ironic that Indigenous people were often not allowed to vote, (but they were welcome to die fighting).[19]

Opposition to US military policies continued despite changes in citizenship status. Chippewa elders of Leech Lake argued that the military draft violated treaties and urged the young not to fight. The Anishinaabeg of Sucker Point, Minnesota, drew up a petition to protest the draft.[20]

To some degree, war participation has varied according to the war. "The Crow Nation is a good illustration of the changing attitudes about the worth of wars. Only 30 Crows served in World War I, compared to 246 in World War II, 135 in Korea, 131 in Vietnam, and only 36 in the Gulf War."[21]

In every war, there have been individuals and communities who have opposed the war and not participated. My father, Vincent LaDuke, was a conscientious objector during the Korean War. He did not feel that it was his war, and his spiritual beliefs as a Native man did not permit him to kill without reason. He was not alone in this belief, not then and not now.

During World War II, the religious and traditional leadership of Zuni Pueblo requested deferments for men who held religious offices. The United Pueblo Agency office in Albuquerque supported the Zuni in this request and many young men were given a 4-D classification for "clergy in training." Nevertheless, over a five-year period of time, a total of 213 Zuni men left their Pueblo for war service, around 10 percent of the population.

The Pueblo leadership continued to petition the military on behalf of those men who had been drafted or enlisted, requesting furloughs so that Zuni soldiers could participate in Shalako and other important traditional ceremonies.

Some believe that the war itself had a positive impact on Zuni ceremonial life as many ceremonies were revitalized through higher attendance and younger leadership was appointed.[22]

The Hopi also maintained conscientious objector status long after the war in 1953, when Thomas Banyaca convinced President Eisenhower that Hopi traditions met this requirement.[23]

In the current conflict in Iraq, a prominent case of conscientious objection came from a Diné Marine named Ronnie Tallman. Despite the high enlistment levels of Navajos in the US Army, religious duty is very important in Navajo society. While home on leave in November 2005, Tallman discovered he had been given the gift of a sacred entity known as *teehn leii.*

Teehn leii is a rare form of spiritual diagnosing and healing called hand-trembling that is known to present itself in Tallman's family. According to Navajo tradition and spiritual law, the gift can neither be acquired nor predicted—it is simply and suddenly bestowed. Diné traditional and spiritual law also holds that Tallman cannot keep the power and serve his people if he participates in killing or war.

Tallman received conscientious objector status after petitioning by the Navajo Medicine Men's Association and by then-president of the Navajo Nation Joe Shirley Jr.

The Diné Hataalii Association, an organization of medicine men recognized by the Navajo Nation, licensed Tallman as a hand-trembler diagnostician. Navajo President Shirley wrote a letter urging Tallman's discharge.

The Tallman application for conscientious objector status received recommendations for approval from several Marine officers over the course of a year before reaching the Conscientious Objector Status Screening Board. An initial disapproval found against Tallman, saying he had failed to provide convincing evidence that his beliefs were "sincere and deeply held." A federal court decision reversed this decision, and the military eventually approved Tallman's request.[24]

THE MILITARY'S TOLL ON THE PEOPLE

When I talk to these young people thinking about going in the military, I tell them, no matter what, the bottom line is you are getting taught to take a human life, that is the skill you're getting taught.
— Charles Sams III, Desert Storm Veteran, interview, May 5, 2010

Wars have taken many of our people and burdened our communities. There is an individual burden borne by soldiers, and there is a burden borne by the communities from which they have come. For those who have served in the military, the weight of their history is heavy. For their communities, the impact of their loss or the changes brought by their return are also significant. Men and women who are involved in killing are changed spiritual beings. In the act of killing you realign your relationship to your relatives.

This taking of life transforms people and permanently changes the perspective you have on the world and on yourself. That is reality. Some of this is positive and some is negative, but in traditional warfare the role of the Ogichidaa was recognized and cared for in a ceremonial manner to address the change of relationships.

Being a veteran and being in the military also change the perceptions of Anglo-American society. In general, interviews indicate that reservation-based Native people see a different attitude from their military peers toward them, different than they would experience in non-military circumstances like in reservation border towns. In the military, they feel greater respect from whites. On the other hand, the institutionalized racism which many veterans face upon their return to the United States, whether in the form of border-town racism, lack of social services or an ongoing set of unjust relations between Native and non-Native society remains a frustrating reality, not only for the individual soldier, but also for the community.

During World War II, Native service men and women described feeling "accepted as an individual, not as one of a minority group." Studies indicate that "this higher level of acceptance, particularly for reservation based Native men and women, meant that racism was not as apparent as in the border towns of home. Interviews with World War II veterans, found that some of the psychological barriers which had always been present in relations between the Indian and the White were torn down."[25]

While explicit racism was muted in the military, it remained a constant force at home. The impact of returning to America and experiencing no change in institutional racism cannot be overstated. Many—as was the case of Navajo Code Talkers in World War II—returned and found that they were unable to vote (eleven states specifically barred Native people from voting until the late 1940s or 1950s), and had difficulty securing loans under the GI Bill. In terms of "white tape" and bureaucracy, neither the Veteran's Administration nor the banks would make a loan on allotment lands or Indian trust lands, barring any entry into the American dream.[26]

One of the most prominent cases of this irony was Ira Hayes, a Pima man who served in World War II and participated in what quickly came to be one of the most iconic images of the war and a universal symbol of pride in military service: the flag raising at Iwo Jima.

The army pulled Ira and two other surviving men who raised the flag at Mt. Suribachi out of combat and pressed them into a bond drive campaign to raise money to pay for the war, touring the country, endlessly raising symbolic flags to replicate the event for the public.

Ira Hayes struggled with his position and the reality of America. (As a note, not a single member of the Pima people served in World War I; nine of seventeen Pima who served in World War II died in combat.)[27] He suffered from PTSD that the military took no interest in diagnosing or treating. He personally rejected the notion that his actions made him a hero when so many "real" heroes had given their lives. His story became legendary with Johnny Cash's recording of *The Ballad of Ira Hayes*.[28]

THE BALLAD OF IRA HAYES

Words and music by Peter LaFarge

Gather round me people there's a story I would tell
About a brave young Indian you should remember well
From the land of the Pima Indian
A proud and noble band
Who farmed the Phoenix valley in Arizona land

Down the ditches for a thousand years
The water grew Ira's peoples' crops
'Till the white man stole the water rights
And the sparklin' water stopped

Now Ira's folks were hungry
And their land grew crops of weeds
When war came, Ira volunteered
And forgot the white man's greed

CHORUS:
Call him drunken Ira Hayes
He won't answer anymore
Not the whiskey drinkin' Indian
Nor the Marine that went to war

There they battled up Iwo Jima's hill,
Two hundred and fifty men
But only twenty-seven lived
to walk back down again

And when the fight was over
And when Old Glory raised
Among the men who held it high
Was the Indian, Ira Hayes

CHORUS

Ira Hayes returned a hero
Celebrated through the land
He was wined and speeched and honored;
Everybody shook his hand

But he was just a Pima Indian
No water, no home, no chance
At home nobody cared what Ira'd done
And when did the Indians dance

CHORUS

Then Ira started drinkin' hard;
Jail was often his home
They'd let him raise the flag and lower it
like you'd throw a dog a bone!

He died drunk early one mornin'
Alone in the land he fought to save
Two inches of water in a lonely ditch
Was a grave for Ira Hayes

Yeah, call him drunken Ira Hayes
But his land is just as dry
And his ghost is lyin' thirsty
In the ditch where Ira died

Call him drunken Ira Hayes
He won't answer anymore
Not the whiskey drinkin' Indian
Nor the Marine that went to war

Ira Hayes on display. Photo: USMC
archives

AMERICAN INDIAN VETERANS
AND POST TRAUMATIC STRESS DISORDER

Unfortunately, American Indian veterans generally suffer from much higher levels of post traumatic stress disorder (PTSD) than veterans from other communities. Indeed, studies of Vietnam veterans found that returning southwestern tribal veterans suffered from post traumatic stress disorder at a rate of 45 percent, while northern Plains tribal veterans returning suffered from PTSD at a rate of 57 percent. This high percentage was largely attributed to the high levels of combat exposure experienced by Native soldiers. In one study, a full 42 percent of those interviewed had seen heavy fighting, some 32 percent had seen medium combat.[29]

The intense mental anguish of PTSD contributes to high rates of suicide among veterans. Anishinaabe veteran Jim Northrup notes that more American service men died from suicide after Vietnam than those who died in "combat."[30]

> My father was a Grunt in Vietnam, my great uncle Calvin survived the first wave of the invasion at Normandy beach, My Grandfather survived his stint as a forward observer in Korea. Crazy Horse survived the wave of attacks from the government to steal the land. . . . The Native American soldier when confronted with the Viet Cong would actually be looking into more of a mirror than if the Native was looking at a fellow United States Soldier. The Native Soldier and the South East Asian soldier have similar tones and colors of skin pigment. They look at each other and see cousins or uncles, they see a resemblance. The government saw the tribal resemblance when looking upon them also. . . . They see Crazy Horse in every Native who is called or volunteers to serve. They also see Crazy Horse in the enemy.

> Guilt can be found among these men as when they searched the bodies of the fallen Crazy Horses of the Viet Cong, it was hard not to notice the similar appearances of these men and Indians. 'He looked like an Indian, he looked like one of my cousins.'

> Crazy Horse sells his medals when he goes broke, buys a dozen beers and drinks them all, tells the bartender he is short on time all the time now. He chances with mortality as though he does

not possess it. The line seems to say he tries to tempt or flirt with death, to bring it close again, to see how close he can bring it to him again. . . . My father would say, 'After the war, it is all gravy son, it's all gravy.' These Veterans speak with guilt and remorse for being the one who made it home, with them they bring the guilt of survival.

The bartender asks him why he is giving up everything he has earned? Crazy Horse tells him you can't stop a man from trying to survive no matter where he is. To Crazy Horse it becomes shameful to have fought against the ones who were 'trying to survive.' ... We are still Crazy Horses.[31]

"America... are you ready for the veterans to come home from this war? As a survivor of the malady called Post Traumatic Stress Disorder, maybe I can help someone who is coming back?"
—*Jim Northrup,*
Fond du Lac Follies

In January of 2010, suicides of active military men and women exceeded combat deaths. During that time period, more soldiers committed suicide (24) than were killed by enemy fire in Afghanistan and Iraq combined (16). In fact, the problem of military suicides is growing much worse, according to Army Chief of Staff George Casey. Casey claimed to be mystified by the suicide rates.[32]

The increasing rate of military suicides is especially disconcerting for Native America because we have both the highest rate of enlistment and the highest rate of living veterans of any ethnic group in the United States. When our people suffer trauma, our communities also suffer trauma.[33]

ON THE REAL PRICE COMBAT VETERANS PAY
By Colonel Anthony DeClue

The combat troop is who I am writing about; they are the ones that come out and feel they don't have a place in society anymore. There have been countless movies and books written about the glory of war, the honor, the excitement, the warrior image. Talk to a veteran that has spent a large amount of time in combat and none of these descriptions will come out of their mouths. If you can get them to talk about it at all you will hear shame, anger, resentment and a lot of confusion.

You have to gain a lot of trust with these individuals before you hear their stories. They have had to live through and see things that don't line up with any society, yet they had to perform these tasks without emotion or a thought of how they will live with it the rest of their lives. Does this determine the rest of their lives? In some instances it does, this is where it becomes an individual again, a choice if you will. How much trauma does one person endure and live? That question is hard to answer.

There are a lot of combat veterans that can't live with their actions and make a choice to take their own lives, whether it be slow by alcohol and drugs or immediate by suicide. Does this make them less of a person? So many of these veterans are highly decorated. So you see how the medals are just a reminder.

Then there are the ones that withdraw totally from society, they live in the bush, they are homeless, they are institutionalized whether in prison or the mental hospitals. Are these people really living? Was this what was in their plan when they took that oath? Is this the price for trying to get a better life, when you grow up in an impoverished situation?

What is the real price us combat veterans pay? We pay many prices, some physical. Bullet wounds, shrapnel wounds, lost body parts, chemical poisoning, spinal cord injuries and the list can go on and on. Any way you can think of tearing apart a human body is possible in war. What about the mental wounds—PTSD, depression, anxiety disorders, flash backs, hallucinations, numerous fears, and on and on. What about the social price? Loss of the family they started before they went to war, loss of friends, loss of children, loss of purpose and on and on. The price is bigger than imagined.

– Interview with retired Colonel Anthony DeClue,
a 26-year combat veteran, Special Forces, March 20, 2009

CEREMONIES AND POWWOWS:
VETERAN RECOGNITION AND HEALING

Dancing at the Grand Forks Wacipi Powwow in 2010, the wars are far away, but they are very present. This is a competition powwow, which draws a thousand or so Native people from the region. Just after the opening grand entry, flag song and veterans' song, there is an Ogichidaa Song, a warrior song. I watch as the elderly Native traditional dancers move slowly in the side step, and dance. The men have brilliant and beautiful beadwork, eagle feathers and regalia. Their bustles sway as they stand and dance in place honoring their history, our history. We all dance to honor our warriors, our veterans. This is how we are healed.

–Winona LaDuke, April 19, 2010

Our ceremonies and our powwows are what likely save many Native veterans.

As Jim Northrup and many other veteran authors and sociologists have found, tribal ceremonies have been a primary source of healing and restoration for their mental and spiritual health.

The recognition of tribal veterans at powwows and veterans' dances has helped dramatically in reintegrating tribal veterans into communities. Native veterans in a cultural and community sense have a much better chance at restoring their own spiritual and mental health than many non-Native veterans, illustrating the strength and integrity of an adapting Native community, as our community collectively seeks to heal from historic trauma.

In short, the impact of military service on individual Native people is dramatic—and all too often traumatic—yet Native communities continue to work very hard to restore the spiritual and physical well-being of our veterans, as well as ensuring their social reintegration and honoring them within community structures.

II.

The Military and the Economy

The US military is preeminent on a worldwide scale, dwarfing the militaries of other nations; it maintains more than 700 army, navy and air force bases around the globe, and operates more large aircraft carriers than the rest of the world combined. To sustain such unparalleled force and global hegemony requires a massive amount of money in continuous, ever-growing streams.

The US defense budget is not only the largest in the world but also significantly larger than the budgets of most of our "enemies" combined. In 2009, the US military budget was nine times larger than China's and comprised about half of total world military expenditures. The United States and its allies comprised around three-quarters of the world's military expenditures, with total global military spending at a whopping $1.7 trillion.[34]

The military budget has to come from somewhere, and especially in an economic downturn the war budget continues to take from other basic human needs, whether early childhood education programs, Indian Health Service, energy assistance or federal housing budgets.

According to the National Priorities Project, Operation Enduring Freedom has cost around $150 billion since 2001, the Afghan and Iraqi war efforts overall are at $1.05 trillion.

The World's Top Five Military Budgets (2009)

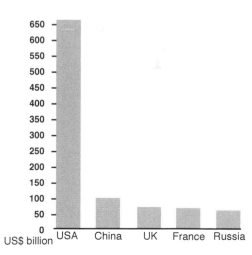

Source: Stockholm International Peace Research Institute (SIPRI).

These figures mean that since 2001, the war has cost us $8,763 per household. As of 2009, the direct US appropriations for the Iraq war, which has lasted longer than World War II, are at $642 billion, and our total defense expenditures are the largest at any point in history, representing up to 48 percent of tax revenues. Compare budgets and Indian Country doesn't even figure.

Global Distribution of Military Expenditure in 2007

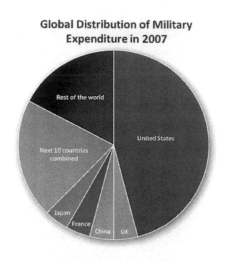

Source: Stockholm International Peace Research Institute Yearbook 2008

The cost of the war includes future costs resulting from current wars. Economists Linda Bilmes and Joseph Stiglitz project that if all the costs of this war are included, like the lifetime of care required for returning troops who are psychologically or physically ill, the cost of the war will be around $3 trillion. In addition, as Lester Brown notes, "the Iraq war may prove to be one of history's most costly mistakes, not so much because of the fiscal outlay but because it has diverted the world's attention from climate change and the other threats to civilization itself."[35]

Considering that ten of the twenty poorest counties in the United States are on Indian reservations, there are some significant infrastructure needs in Native America that could better use the vast resources going to pay for wars.

Veterans have taken note: "Specialist Gerald Dupris of the Cheyenne River reservation and Staff Sergeant Julius Tulley of the Navajo Nation held a news conference to argue that poverty in Indian country was worse than that in Iraq. Both soldiers, along with the Chairman of the National American Indian Housing Council, argued that conditions had worsened as a direct result of the war." As an example, Dupris and Tulley cited that "the Bush administration had cut the federal budget for Native housing from $647 million to $582 million."[36]

At the same time, veterans' benefits represent only a very small portion of the federal military budget and are dwindling. Veterans' benefits provide a somewhat secure revenue stream in impoverished communities and represent a critical part of tribal economies considering the high rate of unemployment in most tribal communities.

While veterans and health and human service programs have all suffered during the economic downturn, it appears weapon sales are recession proof. Despite the global recession of 2008, the United States actually increased arms sales internationally.

According to Thom Shanker of the *New York Times*, in 2008 the United States "expanded its role as the world's leading weapons supplier, increasing its share to more than two-thirds of all foreign armaments deals." Shanker adds that "the United States signed weapons agreements valued at $37.8 billion in 2008, or 68.4 percent of all business in the global arms bazaar, up significantly from American sales of $25.4 billion the year before."[37] Increasing worldwide poverty appears to correspond to an upsurge in the purchase of weapons, and therefore, increased killing and death, all of which benefits the US military economy.

A PERFECT STORM: A NAVAJO CASE STUDY

The Navajo Nation had a high rate of enlistment in the military during

World War II, but also a higher level of rejection for military service, largely because many of the Navajo men only spoke their own language. Later, of course, Navajo speakers provided US forces with a major strategic benefit in the form of the Navajo Code Talkers.

Ironically, at a time when critical military operations and the lives of many thousands depended on the Navajo language, Indian children were still being punished for speaking their language in boarding schools across the United States and Canada.

Navajo Marine, by Monte Singer

NATIVE CODE TALKERS

The military actually used Native Code Talkers from at least 19 tribes,
including Comanche, Cherokee, Choctaw, Lakota, Hopi and Meskwaki, but
the Navajo Code Talkers became the most widely known, inspiring popular
movies and treatments in military histories and textbooks acknowledging
their vital roles in the success of many battles throughout World War II.

Studies and interviews with Navajo veterans found essential transformations of thinking in many of these veterans, which had very significant
impacts upon Navajo society and economics later.

Thousands of Navajo men served in World War II. Most came from very
traditional families whose matrilineal, Indigenous social and spiritual systems were only recently impacted by the Christian churches and boarding
schools and the beginning of the Navajo Livestock Reduction Program.
Acculturation of Navajo veterans was studied by Evon Vogt, John Adair and
Claire Kluckhohn in the 1940s and 1950s, and they developed some theses
as to the social impact of the war on the Navajo Nation.[38]

Complex interviews and research methods with, arguably, the biases of
white sociologists nevertheless revealed a set of trends. Many veterans
returned with a transformed sense of the place of Diné creation, Diné
Natural Law and social structures in the national and international world.
From a society that for millennia understood its place in relationship to the
Holy People, and a pathway to keep that balance, the war added a significant new social lens to veterans' points of view. Many of those interviewed
returned with a new view of "man's mastery" over nature, a very significant
value shift from a perception that the Natural world and Creator's law is preeminent. They had a much more significant future orientation, as opposed
to the present timeframe. The veterans said that the United States was
the most powerful country in the world, and that there was a larger social
universe controlled by various kinds of "white people." Moreover, Navajo
veterans often embraced more individualistic, rather than traditional, social
orientations in relation to community, clan and family.[39]

Navajo veterans participated extensively in Veterans Administration benefits, including both financial and agricultural assistance, with great support
from their tribal leadership. This was, generally, in contrast to Zuni religious and political leadership, which was much more hesitant to have Zuni

veterans continue formal involvement with the outside society.

Consequently, many Navajo veterans continued their training with the military and continued their education in western universities. The benefits and impacts of this education have been dramatic; The Navajo Nation has a high rate of civil and electrical engineers along with unusually large numbers involved in other sciences.

Under what is known as a World War II generation of leadership, most of the coal and uranium mining leases were signed in the Navajo Nation, resulting in hundreds of millions of dollars in royalties from energy corporations and dire environmental and health issues related to extraction.

As Diné investigative journalist and scholar John Redhouse explains: "The white tribal lawyers (Norman Littell, Harold Mott, and George Vlassis) on Navajo were in legal (and in large part, political) power during the main lease signing period of the 1950s through the 1970s. The government boarding school alumni along with WWII veterans made up most of the tribal council members and tribal chairmen of that era."[40]

It was a perfect storm in many ways. Three economic and policy transformations descended upon the Diné people around the same time—the war, the Navajo Livestock Reduction Program and the rise of the nuclear and fossil fuel era.

At the close of stock reduction programs on the Navajo Nation during the 1930s, many Diné were forced from a self-reliant land-based economy into abject poverty. The sizeable recruitment efforts of Navajo were met with enthusiasm, in part, because of the loss of wealth that had just occurred.

The munitions depots at Fort Wingate and Belmont, Arizona employed Diné people, adding another source of war-related income for Navajo families. Over 15,000 soldiers eventually left the Navajo Nation for the military. The soldiers and their families saw checks return to the community and wages paid by the war industry which far surpassed the prices paid to Navajo people for agricultural products at local trading posts or in the rug markets.

In John Adair's reporting on World War II Navajo transitions he notes:

The cash income of the Navajo tribe more than doubled; great quantities of store goods were purchased and most of the weavers laid aside their wool cards and spindles until after the war work and allotment checks 'dried up.' Likewise the Pueblo women gave up their pottery making. . . . It is my conclusion that after having interviewed more than a hundred veterans . . . that the . . . Second World War has exerted a great impact on the cultures of these peoples, perhaps the greatest since the arrival of the Spaniards four hundred years ago.[41]

At the same time as the war transition came the Navajo livestock reduction tragedy, forcing people into dependency and a wage economy. The initial so-called "voluntary stock reduction program" from 1933 to 1935 resulted in the "reduction" of up to 27 percent of Navajo livestock. Additional stock reduction initiatives were forced on the Navajo and by 1952 they had as little as 36 percent remaining of their 1936 stock. In the end, Navajos had lost 80 percent of their per capita holdings.[42]

The sequence of mining leases during this period is also notable. The Bureau of Indian Affairs and the Navajo Tribal Council signed a rapid number of coal and uranium leases during this era, transforming a millennium-old traditional economy into a fossil fuels and nuclear producing economy to meet the needs of America's energy and military expansion.

A book on Navajo uranium miner oral histories points out, "In the 1940s the Navajo Nation was in the early stages of economic development, recovering from the stock reduction period of 1930. Navajo men sought work away from the reservation. . . . Then came the nuclear age and uranium was discovered on the reservation. Work became available and young Navajo men grabbed the jobs in the uranium mines."[43]

By 1987, the Navajo Nation's fossil fuel and uranium-based economy produced over $42 million in royalty revenues, a number that continued to rise, not to mention significant labor revenues. According to the Navajo Nation's Comprehensive Economic Development strategy data:

> [Mining] contributed $53.8 million, $66.5 million, $67.6 million and $71.3 million (unaudited) to the Navajo Nation coffers in the Fiscal Years 2002, 2003, 2004 and 2005 respectively, and was

expected to contribute $56.0 million during the Fiscal Year 2006.[44]

During those years between 2002 and 2005, mining provided 42 57 percent of the revenue for the Navajo Nation General Fund Budget.[45] This percentage has declined in the past few years, with the cessation of operations at the Black Mesa coal mine in 2006 due to the closure of the Mohave Power Plant. The Pittsburgh and Midway mines near Window Rock will also close, leaving the Navajo Nation in need of new revenue sources.[46]

In the 75 years since the Navajo Code Talkers were part of changing world history, the Navajo Nation has been transformed. Today, the Navajo Nation remains in a bitter dilemma and conflict over its continued reliance on an extraction based economy. The militarization of the Navajo economy, however, played a significant role in the transformation of the region.

NATIVE MILITARY CONTRACTORS

A few Native nations and corporations have taken a direct role as military contractors because of Native preference in awarding contracts, with some excellent financial returns. Arguably, this can be a lucrative area of economic development for tribal nations, but it is also a moral liability.

The Department of Defense explains that the Indian Incentive Program "motivates prime contractors to utilize Indian organizations and Indian-owned economic enterprises, by providing a 5% rebate to Prime contractors on subcontracted work performed by an Indian organization or on subcontracted commercial products manufactured in whole or in part by an Indian organization."[47]

An example is Keres Consulting in New Mexico, which in 2009 was awarded a $3.5 million contract by the US Department of Defense for the Native American Lands Environmental Mitigation Program, an initiative that intends to mitigate environmental impacts from DOD activities on Indian lands.[48] They may be busy, as the Department of Defense is the nation's largest toxic polluter, with tens of thousands of toxic "hot spots."[49]

Elsewhere, companies working with the Cherokee Nation in Oklahoma received contracts in 2006 to provide health services to defense workers worth some $20 million. Choctaw Manufacturing, also in Oklahoma, has been contracted to make metal products for the Navy and Army.[50]

Radiance Technologies is a military subcontractor that has also worked with tribal communities. The Advanced Electronic Rosebud Integration plant in Mission, South Dakota is a 10,000 square-foot facility that does testing for the military, employing 12 tribal members, including four veterans, out of 15 total employees. Radiance Technologies has similar partnerships at the Blackfeet and Osage reservations, the former working on composites, and the latter involved with cyberspace security.[51]

The Navajo Nation continues its military contracts with the Raytheon Corporation, in a twenty-year contract, which employs some 330 tribal people. The Raytheon facility is located at Navajo Agricultural Products Industries, and generates substantial local wages. Navajo employees produce weapons systems presently in use by the military. This includes, according to *Indian Country Today*, "Tube-launched, Optically-tracked, Wire-guided (TOW) missile; Javelin Close Combat/Anti-armor Weapon System; Stinger; Phalanx Close-In Weapon System and Excalibur Precision Guided Extended Range Artillery Projectile."[52] In 2009, Raytheon changed the name of its facility to Raytheon Diné, to reflect a connection to local heritage.[53]

LARGEST PRIVATE ARMY IN THE WORLD: A NATIVE CONTRACTOR

Little did we know that the largest private army in the world was actually a Native American contractor. That would be Blackwater, and it is subcontracting for the Chenega Native Corporation (Alaskan Native). Chenega is a tribal corporation utilizing Native preference to secure a contract for a non-Native enterprise with the intent of creating a revenue stream for a tribal community.

Chenega Native Corporation, which originally had 69 shareholders, has a diversified base of operations, with offices in Alaska and Virginia. A report prepared for a US Senate Subcommittee on contracting oversight found that "Between 2000 and 2008, Chenega Corporation's federal contract awards increased 4,190%, from $9.6 million in 2000 to $412.9 million in 2008. Over the last nine years, Chenega was awarded federal prime contracts totaling more than $1.9 billion."[54]

Alaskan author Stuart Archer Cohen explains the Chenega/Blackwater relationship, "Chenega gets contracts through the Small Business

Administration, rakes off a percentage, and then lets giant Blackwater provide the actual services. Since 2000 Chenega has received over $1.1 billion in sole-source or non-compete bids from the Army, Air Force and Department of Homeland Security."[55] These kinds of contracts are largely the result of rules crafted by recently defeated (amidst corruption charges), very powerful former Alaska Senator, Ted Stevens.

A bit about the corporation formerly known as Blackwater: it was renamed Xe Services, and now it is called Academi. For those unfamiliar with this corporation, Blackwater has been the largest private security firm in the world, and has a wide range of assets as well as liabilities, including a myriad of legal problems associated with using excessive force against Iraqi civilians.

Blackwater personnel were charged with illegally killing a number of Iraqi civilians in 2004. The shootings sparked at least five investigations, and an FBI probe found that Blackwater employees used lethal force recklessly. However, in January of 2010, the five Blackwater employees charged with the killings were released, their convictions overturned on technical aspects of the trial, which the court ruled had violated their civil rights.

Two former Blackwater contractors were recently convicted of involuntary manslaughter and sentenced to prison for killing Iraqi civilians in 2009, after an earlier murder trial resulted in a hung jury.

US District Court Judge Robert Doumar spoke critically of Blackwater, saying "They [Blackwater] have a responsibility to hire individuals who they feel are capable of following orders and not going off on some tear."[56] And of the two convicted contractors, the judge said "They tried to paint their victims as aggressors, and they weren't aggressors. . . . They were just victims."[57]

Four more former Blackwater contractors face manslaughter charges stemming from a 2007 shooting incident in Baghdad that left 17 Iraqi civilians dead.

Blackwater/XE is also facing a $60 million class-action lawsuit for allegedly depriving its workers of employee benefits to which they are entitled.

According to the lawsuit (filed on behalf of more than 3,000 people who have done security work for the company in Iraq, Afghanistan and elsewhere since 2001), Blackwater/XE improperly classified the workers as independent contractors rather than employees, failed to pay Social Security taxes and failed to contribute to state unemployment funds or provide health, disability or pension plans. The lawsuit claims that many workers have come home from war zones physically or psychologically wounded and have been denied health care because of the alleged misclassification.[58]

III.

The Military and the Land

The Mother Earth provides us with food, provides us with air, provides us with water. We, the people, are going to have to put our thoughts together, to save our planet here. We've only got one water, one air, one Mother Earth. Let's take care of her and she will take care of us
— Corbin Harney, Western Shoshone spiritual leader and peace activist.

The US military is the largest polluter in the world. If one begins to consider the whole of the impact of the US military on the planet, historically and in the present, it is, in fact, damning.

From the more than a thousand nuclear weapons tests in the Pacific and the Nevada desert that started in the 1940s, obliterating atolls and spreading radioactive contamination throughout the ocean and across large areas in the American West, to the Vietnam War-era use of napalm and Agent Orange to defoliate and poison vast swaths of Vietnam, to the widespread use of depleted uranium and chemical weaponry since that time, the role of the US military in contaminating the planet cannot be overstated.

WHAT FALLS UPON MOTHER EARTH, FALLS UPON HER CHILDREN

The United States military nearly drowned much of Southeast Asia with poisons sprayed from the air during its war with Vietnam.

Under a program called Operation Ranch Hand, the US military sprayed some 20 million gallons of chemical herbicides and defoliants in Vietnam, eastern Laos and parts of Cambodia, much of that contaminated with dioxin, a known human carcinogen. The chemicals were sprayed indiscriminately, whether people were in the vicinity or not, over crops and food supplies, even over US troops in the field.

Agent Orange is the most commonly used and widely remembered of the several deadly toxic compounds that the military used during the course of the war. Others were code-named Agent Pink, Agent Blue, Agent White, Agent Green, and Agent Purple.

About 10 percent of the trees sprayed died from a single spray run. Multiple spraying resulted in increased mortality for the trees and undergrowth, as did following the herbicide missions with napalm or bombing strikes.[59]

During the ten years of spraying, over 5 million acres (20,000 km²) of forest and 500,000 acres (2,000 km²) of crops were heavily damaged or destroyed. Around 20 percent of the forests of South Vietnam were sprayed at least once.[60]

While the US military thought perhaps that the chemical weaponry would be a good strategy for waging war against the Vietnamese, the poisons remain in Vietnam to this day, affecting countless thousands of Vietnamese civilians. The legacy of these poisons also came home to America with the soldiers.

F-100D dropping a napalm bomb in South Vietnam. Photograph courtesy of the National Museum of the US Air Force.

REMEMBERING OGICHIDAA BILLY WALKABOUT

Photo courtesy of the family of Billy Walkabout

"War is not hell," Walkabout said. "It's worse."

Billy Walkabout (1949–2007) was one of the most-decorated soldiers of the Vietnam War era, having received the Distinguished Service Cross, five Silver Stars, ten Bronze Stars and six Purple Hearts.

A Cherokee of the Blue Holley Clan, he was an 18-year-old Army Ranger sergeant when he and 12 other soldiers were sent on a mission behind enemy lines where they came under fire for hours, during which he was seriously wounded. Several of the squad were killed at the scene, while the rest later died of their injuries.

His Distinguished Service Cross commendation stated that Billy Walkabout simultaneously returned fire, helped his comrades and boarded other injured soldiers onto evacuation helicopters. "Although stunned and wounded by the blast, Sgt. Walkabout rushed from man to man administering first aid, bandaging one soldier's severe chest wound and reviving another soldier by heart massage. Only when the casualties had been evacuated and friendly reinforcements had arrived, did he allow himself to be evacuated."[61]

He retired as a second lieutenant. In a 1986 interview with the Associated Press, Walkabout said his 23 months in Vietnam left him with disabling injuries and memories that refused to fade.

From Billy Walkabout's journal, soul-words in his own voice:

> I shipped out to Vietnam. I wanted to serve my nation and protect my people. I found myself in the jungles of Vietnam, ten thousand miles from home. Under monsoon rains, under a

painted sky, leeches crawled on my arms. The little blood-suckers
fell off into the night. The rain fell all night.

Back in the world, no gal danced the southern dance for me. And
the clouds hid the sun. I was burdened with separation from my
family and the rez. I couldn't wear an eagle feather on my steel-
helmet or tear that peace sign away. My war-shirt had blood all
over it. I had blood on my hands. I saw people die. I saw medevac
helicopters air lift them out. Those guys would remain in my
memory. I didn't have time to grieve then. Firebase on the distant
mountain. The jungle was full of mountain ghosts.

Sweet Lady, I never had your love to get me through, nor did I
ever receive any of your letters. You still were so far and so many
years away on the great turtle island. I had to go through a year of
combat.

I came home to a hostile and ungrateful nation. I was treated
like a war-criminal. I felt like I didn't even belong in this land of
my ancestors, and all the way through, I was a wounded warrior
struggling with PTSD. I tried to get back on track, but I had too
many 'nam flashbacks. Not even Ojibwe dreamcatchers could
catch all the nightmares. There were years of drug use, alcohol-
ism, homelessness, and racism, before I found my way to you.[62]

He was awaiting a kidney transplant at the time of his death at the age of 58,
the legacy of Agent Orange exposure and a military in many ways indiffer-
ent to the impact of its weaponry on its own soldiers.

DEPLETED URANIUM

Over the last fifty years of enriching uranium for nuclear power plants
and weapons, the United States has accumulated around 500,000 tons of
depleted uranium (DU).

Jim Harding, in *Canada's Deadly Secret: Saskatchewan Uranium and the
Global Nuclear System,* writes:

Some clever arms industry researchers invented a means to use
this to make a profitable military product. This can be seen as the

military-industrial complex's perverted version of recycling.

> Because uranium is the heaviest element on the planet, the
> arms researchers came up with the not so complicated idea that
> bombs containing uranium could be used to pierce less dense
> metals like the steel casing on tanks. It was a classically destruc-
> tive engineering feat, with no consideration of what happens
> when a DU bullet hits a target and disperses radiation on the
> ground and into the atmosphere.[63]

DU weapons became mass-produced by the 1990s.[64]

The United States has launched, detonated and lost hundreds of tons of
weapons containing depleted uranium over the course of several Gulf
Wars. Depleted uranium shells have 60 percent of the original radioactivity of normal uranium, so it's a rather large mess, and has caused widespread radioactive contamination of not only soldiers but also civilians and
the land. Since 1995, this practice has been condemned by international
human rights agencies and the United Nations as a form of biological weaponry, with long term implications, far past the immediate war effort. The
military, however, has continued to use depleted uranium weaponry.

In 2006, the military command at Schofield Barracks Base in Hawaii admit-
ted that it had been using depleted uranium weaponry in Hawaii. Despite
reassurances to the contrary, freedom of information document releases
revealed that DU had been used.[65] "The Army was forced to disclose information to the public about the DU contamination and have conducted
studies and environmental monitoring. The Army revealed that the source
of the DU was a classified nuclear weapon called the 'Davy Crockett' Light
Weapon M28. The Davy Crockett was made to fire the Mk-54 warhead,
which weighed about 51 lb (23 kg), with a selectable yield of 10 or 20 tons."[66]

A contractor hired to clean up Schofield reported, "We have found much
that we did not expect, including recent find of depleted uranium. We are
pulling tons of frag and scrap out of the craters in the western area to the
point where it has basically turned into a manual sifting operation. Had this
not been a CWM [Chemical Warfare Material] site, we would have moved
mechanical sifters in about 5 weeks ago but the danger is just too high."[67]

In the end, one is left with the conclusion that the US military has ruthlessly scorched the earth as a part of routine, embedded and historic military practice.

THE URANIUM, ATOMIC WEAPONS AND DEPLETED URANIUM CONNECTION

He had been so close to it, caught up in it for so long that its sim-plicity struck him deep inside his chest: Trinity Site, where they exploded the first atomic bomb, was only three hundred miles to the southeast, at White Sands. And the top-secret laboratories where the bomb had been created were deep inside the Jemez Mountains, on land the Government took from Cochiti Pueblo: Los Alamos, only a hundred miles northeast of him now, still sur-rounded by high electric fences and the ponderosa pine and tawny sand rock of the Jemez mountain canyon where the shrine of the twin mountain lions had always been. There was no end to it. It knew no boundaries. . . . From the jungles of his dreaming he rec-ognized why the Japanese voices had merged with Laguna voices. . . . From that time on, human beings were one clan again, united by 'the fate the destroyers had planned for all of them for all living things' united by a circle of death that devoured people in cities twelve thousand miles away, victims who had never known these mesas, who had never seen the delicate colors of the rocks which boiled up their slaughter.

– Excerpted from the novel *Ceremony*, by Leslie Marmon Silko

On a worldwide scale, Native people hold around 70 percent of the world's uranium resources—from the north of Saskatchewan, to the Diné and other Indigenous territories of the southwest, the Lakota Nation to the Mirarr nation of Australia.

Despite a 30-year hiatus from building new nuclear power plants in the United States, there is intense pressure to reboot the nuclear industry and, in the process, restart uranium mining operations in Native America. All of this is of serious concern to Native people.

Over 1,000 uranium mines gouged the earth in the area of the Diné Bikeyah— the land of the Navajo, during a 30-year period, beginning in the 1950s. Those mines, the largest uranium mine in the world at the time, at Laguna Pueblo, mines on the Spokane and near the Pine Ridge reservation are part of the uranium industry's deadly legacy in Native America. The lethal nature of the uranium industry led it to the isolated lands of Native America.

Indeed, as the Los Alamos Scientific Laboratory would note in 1978, "perhaps the solution to the radon emission problem is to zone the land into uranium mining and milling districts so as to forbid human habitation."[68]

By the mid 1970s, there were 380 uranium leases on Native land and only four on public or acquired lands. Not only are Indigenous peoples' territories underlain by uranium, but the industry and government were fully aware of the health impacts of uranium mining on workers, their families and the land upon which their descendents would come to live.

The uranium used "to boil up their slaughter" likely came from a variety of sources, whether Tayo's blessed Laguna Pueblo, or El Dorado's Port Radium Mine in the Northwest Territories.[69]

In all cases, Indigenous people of the Americas are linked to the Hiroshima and Nagasaki bombs, as well as to more than a thousand nuclear tests undertaken in the Pacific and in Nevada.

DOMESTIC WARS

The Department of Defense states that as part of carrying out its mission to defend America, "certain activities—such as weapons testing, practice bombing and field maneuvers—may have had effects on tribal environmental health and safety as well as tribal economic, social and cultural welfare."[70] That would be an understatement.

The US military is one of the largest landowners in the United States, with some 30 million acres of land under its control. The US federal government is the largest landowner in the United States, with much of this land base annexed or otherwise stolen from Native peoples.

The states with the top two federal land holdings are Nevada with 84.5 percent of the state, and Alaska at 69.1 percent of the state being held by the federal government. These represent takings under the 1863 Ruby Valley Treaty with the Shoshone, and the Alaskan Native Claims Settlement Act of 1971. The military controls a large percentage of Hawaii as well, including some 25 percent of Oahu, valuable "submerged lands" (i.e., estuaries and bays), and until relatively recently, the island of Kaho'olawe. The army seized the entire island of Kaho'olawe after the attack on Pearl Harbor. This island was the only national historic site also used as a bombing range. The military reigns over more than 200,000 acres of Hawaii, with over 100 military installations, and at least 150,000 personnel.[71]

SEIZING LAND IN THE NAME OF NATIONAL SECURITY

As of 1916, the US Army owned approximately 1.5 million acres. Land ownership grew by 33 percent in the course of the World War I mobilization. As of 1940, the army owned approximately 2 million acres. The scale of World War II mobilization was unprecedented: the army (including the Army Air Force) acquired 8 million additional acres, thereby quintupling land ownership. Military agencies were given nearly unlimited spending authority to acquire land from private owners and had the option of foreclosing on lands it deemed necessary to national security.[72]

Most of the new acreage cost the army practically nothing. More than 6 million acres, more than three quarters of the land it acquired, came from the public domain.[73]

What is clear is that "public domain" is often really, truthfully Native land. Some of these land transfers came early from Native people. The army took some 10,000 acres from the Cheyenne and Arapaho people for Fort Reno in 1881, and until 1993 had use of Zuni and Navajo lands near Fort Wingate.

In fact, much of what is today US military land was at some time taken from Native peoples, sometimes at gunpoint, sometimes in the wake of massacres or forced marches, sometimes through starvation, and sometimes through pen and paper, broken treaty, acts of Congress or state legislatures, or by presidential authority, by the "Great White Father" himself.

As weapons became more lethal—as harmful to those manufacturing, handling or storing these materials as they would be against an enemy—access to more isolated lands became a major military priority. With the massive increases of chemical, biological and nuclear weaponry that took place during

establishment, newspaper publishers, the military and many others. However, Alaska Natives organized to protest this desecration in 1961, beginning with the Inupiat village at Point Hope, which is located just 30 miles from the intended blast, and successfully stopped this crazy idea.

> By now most are aware of Project Chariot, a project dating from the 1950s that envisioned the use of nuclear detonations to build a harbor at Cape Thompson, Alaska. This was part of the old Plowshare or 'Atoms for Peace' program. Although the nuclear detonations were never carried out, 26 millicuries of radioactive tracers left over from ecological experiments were deposed of at the site. When news of these disposed radioactive tracers broke, the headlines told of a nuclear waste 'dump.' The worst fears of the local people living near Cape Thompson were awakened.[80]

Point Hope, Alaska: Secret Radiation Testing
With the creation of the Plowshare Program, the AEC took radioactive materials from the Nevada test site on Western Shoshone land and secretly placed them in a number of test plots near the Inupiat Eskimo Village of Point Hope.

The purpose of this 1962 experiment was to document and study the effects of radiation bioaccumulation in caribou, lichen and humans in the Arctic. Over 15,000 pounds of radioactive soil were secretly placed in a number of locations in the area.

The 450 residents of Point Hope had never been informed of the testing. The study was inadvertently discovered in a 1992 Freedom of Information request on radioactive experimentation spearheaded by the Department of Energy. The village, along with organizations nationally, including Honor the Earth, pressured the DOE for cleanup, and won.[81]

Fort Greely, Alaska, and the VX Lake
At Fort Greely, Alaska, the military operated a nuclear power plant that ran on highly enriched weapons grade uranium. Originally built to house six anti-ballistic missile silos, the army also used the area for extensive, and one might say chaotic, testing of chemical and biological weaponry.

Although the base has been closed, the nuclear reactor remains entombed on-site and significant contamination is certain to persist for a very long time.[82]

HOMELAND SECURITY AND THE VX LAKE

In the summer of 1969 the Army drained a small lake in interior Alaska. Though this presumably is not something that occurs every day, the event would be unremarkable except for one thing: From the bottom of the lake the Army recovered about two hundred artillery shells and rockets filled with nerve gas.

The lethal weapons had been left on the frozen surface of the lake at Fort Greely's Gerstle River test site during the winter some years earlier. According to the Army, the chemical-filled munitions were scheduled for destruction when they were placed on the ice, but somehow the order to destroy them was never given. Apparently forgotten, the deadly stockpile sank to the bottom when the ice melted under the bright May sun.

The poison gas weapons sank in 1966 and remained in the lake for more than three years before they were retrieved. The Army has not explained why such dangerous material were handled so care-lessly, nor why the loss of a large quantity of nerve gas went unno-ticed for so long. After reports of missing nerve gas weapons finally came to the attention of Arctic Test Center authorities, the Army decided to drain the lake in order to remove the weapons.

The lost chemical weapons were part of the secret CBW program conducted under the aegis of Fort Greely's Arctic Test Center. This bizarre incident is only part of the evidence showing that the pro-tective blanket of national security that shrouds the CBW program elsewhere has concealed the Alaska CBW test activities from the public eye. The story of the lake was unraveled with the story of CBW in Alaska. Together they make a case study in the secrecy with which the CBW program has been managed—and mismanaged.

After the mishap was discovered, the servicemen were instructed to refer to the lake as 'Blueberry Lake.' Though this pleasantly bucolic name is now the official one, it has never caught on among the GIs who knew it as VX Lake.

— Richard A. Fineberg in *The Dragon Goes North: Chemical and Biological Warfare Testing in Alaska* (Santa Barbara, CA: McNally & Loftin, 1972)

PCB Contamination in Alaska

Although less long term in their impact, the persistence of organic pollutants in the Arctic is more pervasive. The Distant Early Warning (DEW) Line consisted of some 63 separate military radar sites along the 66th parallel in Alaska, Canada and Greenland. These sites, although no longer in use, are heavily contaminated with polychlorinated biphenyls (PCBs), which are toxic and carcinogenic. PCBs and other bioaccumulative pollutants in the Arctic have been a major threat to the health of people, polar bears and all life forms. Studies completed in many of the sites in the north indicate that "no consumption" should occur of fish downstream from these sites.[83]

WESTERN SHOSHONE: NUCLEAR TESTING AND NUCLEAR WASTE

> *The food that my people survived on is not here no more on account of this nuclear weapon that we have developed. . . . The pine nuts aren't here no more, the chokecherries aren't here, the antelope aren't here, the deer aren't here, the groundhog aren't here, the sage hen aren't here.*
> — Corbin Harney, Naraya Cultural Preservation Council website

In 1940, President Roosevelt created with a stroke of his pen the single largest gunnery range in the world; the 3.5 million acre Nellis Range. After World War II, this bombing range would be absorbed into the nuclear weapons complex concentrated in Nevada, which has been described as the largest peacetime militarized zone on earth . . . really wasn't good for anything but gunnery practice—you could bomb it into oblivion and never notice the difference.[84]

The Western Shoshone would disagree.

In 1951, the Atomic Energy Commission created its Nevada Test Site within Western Shoshone Territory as proving grounds for nuclear weapons. Between 1951 and 1992, the United States and Great Britain exploded 1,054 nuclear devices both above and below ground there.

Radiation emanating from these experiments was fully measured for only 111 of the tests, about 10 percent of the total.

Within just the first three years, 220 above ground tests spewed fallout over a large area, to be carried by the prevailing winds. The government maintained that the maximum radiation exposure from the tests was equivalent to that of a single chest X-ray. However, in 1997 the National Cancer Institute made public a study of radiation exposure from above ground nuclear tests showing that some 160 million people had suffered significant radiation exposure from the tests, on average 200 times more than the amount indicated by the government.

In some parts of the country, the exposure was found to be 2,000–3,000 times that amount. The institute estimated that as many as 75,000 cases of thyroid cancer may have been caused by atmospheric testing.

None of that is news to Virginia Sanchez, a Western Shoshone woman who grew up in the shadow of the Nevada test site. "When the nuclear tests were exploded, in school we would duck and cover under the desk, not really understanding what it was," she said.[85]

Virginia's brother Joseph Sanchez died of leukemia at 36, and she has lost many relatives. The Western Shoshone communities were directly downwind of the site. Virginia recalls:

> We weren't wealthy, you know our structures weren't airtight. Besides, our people spent major amounts of time outside, picking berries, hunting, gathering our traditional foods … At that time, we still ate a lot of jackrabbits … In Duckwater, which, as the crow flies, is 120 miles direct north of the test site, the people in that community didn't have running water or electricity as a whole community until the early 1970s, so they would gather water outside. So we received some major doses of radiation … The scientists figured that a one-year-old child who ate a contaminated rabbit within a month's time after the test probably had six times the dose of what the DOE's figures were saying … There was a county school about three miles from the reservation, and all the kids wore the film badges (issued by federal officials to document the gamma rays) and they were never told the results.[86]

The MX Missile site and the Yucca Mountain Nuclear Waste Repository were also proposed for Western Shoshone Territory. Both were defeated.

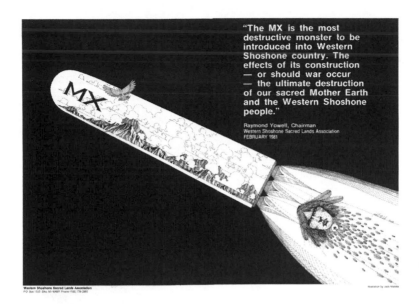

"The MX is the most destructive monster to be introduced into Western Shoshone country. The effects of its construction — or should war occur — the ultimate destruction of our sacred Mother Earth and the Western Shoshone people."

Raymond Yowell, Chairman
Western Shoshone Sacred Lands Association
FEBRUARY 1981

Art by Jack Malotte

NATIVE HAWAII

Makua and Kaho'olawe

> *"They bombed the houses in the 1940s. And took over the entire valley," Sparky Rodrigues explains, one of many Makua, Hawaii residents still waiting to move home. "The government moved all of the residents out and said after the war, you can move back. Then they used the houses for target practice. The families tell stories that the military came to the families with guns, and said, 'Here's $300 thank you' and 'you got to move.' Those people remain without their houses, and for years, many lived on the beaches in beautiful Makua Valley, watching their farms and land get bombed."*
> — Sparky Rodrigues, Interview January 2001

Live ammunition occasionally washes up on the beaches at Makua.

Malu Aina, a military watchdog group from Hawaii, reports, "Live military ordnance in large quantities has been found off Hapuna Beach and in Hilo Bay. Additional ordnance, including grenades, artillery shells, rockets, mortars, armor piercing ordnance, bazooka rounds, napalm bombs, and hedgehog missiles have been found at Hilo airport, in Waimea town, Waikoloa Village, in North and South Kohala at Puako and Mahukona, in Kea'au and Maku'u Farm lots in Puna, at South Point in Ka'u, and on residential

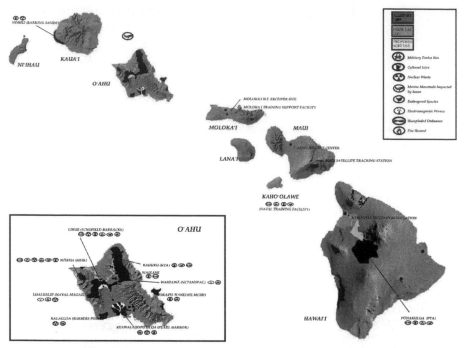

The military controls 236,303 acres in Hawai'i or 5.7 percent of the total land area.
Map courtesy of http://www.dmzhawaii.org/, map created by Summer Mullins.

and school grounds. At least nine people have been killed or injured by exploding ordnance. Some unexploded ordnance can be set off even by cell phones. It's an ongoing problem of expanding military opala [garbage] locally and globally."[87]

Since the end of World War II, Hawaii has been the center of the US military's Pacific Command (PACOM), from which all US forces in the region are directed. It serves as an outpost for Pacific expansionism, along with Guam, the Marshall Islands, Samoa and the Philippines. PACOM is the center of the US military activities over more than half the Earth, from the west coast of the United States to Africa's east coast, from the Arctic to Antarctica, covering 70 percent of the world's oceans.

The island of Kaho'olawe was the only national historic site also used as a bombing range. Finally, after years of litigation and negotiations Congress placed a moratorium on the bombing, but after $400 million in cleanup money, much remains to be completed.[88]

Among the largest military sites in Hawaii is the Pohakuloa Training Area (PTA), a 108,793 acre bombing range between the sacred mountains of Mauna Kea and Mauna Loa in the center of the big island, Hawaii. At least 7 million rounds of ammunition are fired annually at that base alone. The military proposes to expand the base by 23,000 acres, under the Military Transformation Proposal, and has a plan to bring in Stryker brigades to the area. The military is hoping to acquire up to 79,000 more acres in total—so far.[89]

Military Impact on Hawaiian
Endangered Species and Archaeological Sites

Pohakuloa has the "highest concentration of endangered species of any Army installation in the world" according to its former commander Lt. Col. Dennis Owen, and it has over 250 ancient Hawaiian archaeological sites. Those species and archaeological sites are pretty much "toast" under the expansion plans.

In one recent report, the military determined that there were over 236 former military sites in Hawaii at 46 separate installations, all of which were contaminated. These sites, identified under the Formerly Used Defense Sites Program (FUDS) may be condemned by the military to avoid cleanup and liability.[90]

There is no way to avoid an observation. It is as a result of our nation's history of colonialism, its Doctrine of Manifest Destiny and the subsequent expansion of military interests to support American imperialism that Indian Country communities are located adjacent to more than our fair share of these military toxic sites.

This is because many of today's US military bases are the legacy of old US cavalry forts, places where the army built strongholds to support their invasions of Indian Country, places that were used to subjugate and imprison Native people.

The impact of the US military on Indigenous populations extends far beyond the shores of the United States. Take, for example, Guam, where first European and currently American military might has been forced upon the islanders for more than 500 years.

MILITARY BUILDUP IN GUAM
By Sheryl Day

Guam is the largest and southernmost island in the Marianas Islands. The Chamorro people have lived there for over 4,000 years. First contact with Spain occurred in 1521, when Spanish explorers mistook the island for the Indies. Spain declared the island a possession in 1565 and formally occupied Guam from 1668 until 1898, when after its defeat in the Spanish-American War, it ceded the island to the United States under the Treaty of Paris.

Guam became of vital military interest during the course of World War II, first invaded by the Japanese in 1941 and reclaimed by the US military in 1944.

According to the CIA World Factbook, "the military installation on the island is one of the most strategically important US bases in the Pacific."[91]

In 2005, the United States and Okinawa agreed to a "realignment of forces [to] include the Marine move to Guam, which will allow for the consolidation of Marine forces and return to Japan the use of 'significant land.'"[92] This move was due, in part, to the long-standing social, environmental and cultural frictions between the Okinawans and the military base located in Futenma.

Demonstrators protest US military presence in Guam. Photograph by Hermon Farahi.

There are the poisons, and then there is the justice issue. The Nisqually people have a right to a land base that will support their community. That land base historically encompassed Fort Lewis.

Alan Frazier, former Nisqually Tribal Administrator, explained:

> I think there's still an outstanding issue around that land theft that's never been resolved. That is, if they can try to destroy the tribe, shatter the tribe, how can they contribute to bringing the tribe back together? That took 3,500 acres of the heart of the reservation. Rich farmland, agricultural land, people had horses and cattle and were self-sufficient. Somehow we need to, if the tribe is going to survive for thousands more years, we're gonna need some land around here. They say that land is polluted with guns and bullets . . . but still, they've got all kinds of land here. The authorities should give the tribe five or ten thousand acres all around us right here as we speak.
>
> The tribe was kind enough, I guess, to not fight them again. Nisqually could have gone to war again with them. They went to war several times. They went to war on the fishing rights, and went to war when Stevens tried to push that treaty through. We might go to war some other time.[103]

HANFORD NUCLEAR RESERVATION AND THE YAKAMA NATION

> It is estimated that the production and storage of nuclear materials at the site since it opened in 1944 has resulted in exposure levels to those living in the area equivalent to those of the Chernobyl disaster.[104]

The Hanford Nuclear Reservation is the largest nuclear waste dump in the Western Hemisphere and a serious environmental issue in the Northwest. The Hanford complex is located entirely within the treaty boundary of the Yakama Nation.

> Hanford covers 560 square miles of high brush lands in eastern Washington, along 51 miles of the Columbia River. . . . From 1943 to 1988, Hanford produced plutonium for nuclear weapons, using a line of nuclear reactors along the river. Cooling water from the river

was piped through the reactors, then fed back into the river. Spent fuel rods from the reactors were dissolved in nitric acid to separate out the plutonium. Enormous amounts of highly radioactive and chemical waste were generated in the process. Since the production of plutonium ceased, Hanford's only mission has been cleanup.

About 53 million gallons of high-level radioactive and chemical waste are stored in 177 underground tanks the size of three-story buildings, buried in Hanford's central area, about 12 miles from the river. Over the years 70 of the tanks have leaked about one million gallons of waste into the soil. At least some of the leaked tank waste has reached the groundwater, which eventually flows into the river. Estimated time for the tank waste to reach the river is anywhere from 7 to 20 years to a couple of generations. How badly it damages the river depends on how much gets there and when.

Presently DOE does not have a plan for intercepting the tank waste before the waste reaches the river. To prevent more leaks, DOE has been pumping liquid waste out of the leaking single shell tanks into the newer, not yet leaking, double shell tanks.

The long-term plan is to 'vitrify' the waste by combining it with molten glass to produce glass logs which will be stored in a dry underground vault in Hanford's central area. The vitrification plant is now being built.[105]

The Yakama Nation, along with allies at the Columbia River Intertribal Fish Commission, has worked diligently for several decades to begin remediation of this massive nuclear dump. At present, some of the heated water in a cooling tank, which is not radioactive, is being used by the Yakama Nation to rear salmon for release into the river.

UMATILLA CHEMICAL DEPOT AND THE CONFEDERATED TRIBES OF UMATILLA

For 12,000 years, the Umatilla, Wasco, Cayuse and Walla Walla have lived in the Columbia Plateau on lands and waters which sustained their people.

In 1850, however, Congress passed the Oregon Donation Land Act, exclusively for the benefit of white "settlers" and "pioneers," and thereby created the largest land giveaway in the history of the nation, at the sole expense of Native people, who paid with their lives by the thousands.

Decimated by the repeated epidemics the newcomers brought into the region, and relentlessly harassed and murdered by both US Army troops and bloodthirsty white vigilantes, surviving remnants were forced to sign treaties under egregious terms in 1855 and 1856.

White settlers and pioneers had already stolen 2.5 million acres of land in the Oregon Territory by 1856, but even that would not be enough, and the United States was already well established in the habit of unilateral treaty-breaking.

In 1940 the army selected a 16,000 acre parcel from within this territory to become the Umatilla Ordnance Depot. Beginning in 1941, some 7,000 workers were hired and $35 million was spent to create a complex of military storehouses, housing and ammunition. The munitions that were stored there were used in the Korean Conflict, Vietnam, Grenada, Panama, Operation Desert Shield and Operation Desert Storm. In 1962, chemical nerve agents VX and GM and the mustard blister agent HD were sent there.

In the 1980s, Congress began the disposal of the aging chemical weapons stockpile and ratified the UN Convention on Chemical Weapons. At that time, the Umatilla Chemical Agent Disposal Facility was constructed. The destruction of chemical weapons has continued since this time and lands similar to those under discussion elsewhere (Fort Wingate) are subject to recovery by the tribe and other communities. In the meantime the facility has spread to over 19,000 acres of Confederated Tribes of Umatilla Land.[106]

THE MILITARIZATION OF THE US / MEXICO BORDER

The 2.8 million acre Tohono O'odam reservation spans the United States/ Mexico border, with over 75 miles of international territory, but that is just the beginning of Indigenous territories in the region. The Kickapoo people have lands on the borders, and many Indigenous communities (Yaqui and others) consider simply that the "border crossed us."

The militarization of the US/Mexico border is at historic levels, and grows each year—a complex set of dynamics involving drug and human trafficking, weapons smuggling, issues and attitudes regarding immigration, and economic and environmental depredations.

According to a 2009 report from the US Government Accounting Office, this border fencing costs an average of $1 million to $4 million dollars a mile, with some sections costing as much as $15 million per mile. These costs pertain to a 20 to 25 year life expectancy of the fence, which would have to be constantly rebuilt every couple of decades.

Some of these barriers cease to exist at the Tohono O'odam territory. There a five-strand barbed wire fence and cattle guards mark a border which makes little sense to a people who have lived there for thousands of years.

The border is intensely militarized by armed vigilante groups and paramilitary forces, the drug cartels and other criminal enterprises (who use military-grade weaponry), a complex array of law enforcement, border patrol and immigration agencies, and increasing numbers of the American and Mexican military assets and resources.

The 2012 Presidential campaigns (and many undercards) are riddled with candidates' promises to fence and fortify the entire United States/Mexico border. Bills and ballot measures are on legislative and congressional agendas virtually everywhere. GOP audiences cheered Herman Cain's talk at an October 2011 campaign rally about electrifying the southern border fence, unashamedly: "It's going to be 20 feet high. It's going to have barbed wire on the top. It's going to be electrified. And there's going to be a sign on the other side saying, 'It will kill you.'" Recent allocations include about $600 million in predator drones, with a price tag of as much as $32 million apiece. Everything seems to be on the table, including mine fields, flame throwers and maybe a moat.

That is the high end of militarization. The lower end is the weapons trade— the vast majority originating from US weapons dealers.

A Congressional Research Service report released in 2011 found that of the 29,284 weapons confiscated from Mexican drug cartels in 2009–10, 70 percent had originated from US weapons dealers. The "low end of weapons" included anti-armor sniper rifles and armor piercing handguns.

Mexican President Felipe Calderón blasted American authorities, stating, "I accuse the US weapons industry of [responsibility for] the deaths of thousands of people that are occurring in Mexico."[107] Over the past decade, more than 23,000 people have died along the border—some from dehydration and exposure, but many thousands from grisly murders by drug- and human-trafficking cartels.[108]

GETTING YOUR HOMELAND BACK FROM THE MILITARY

Recovery of lands from the military/industrial complex is a bit complicated. As it is, under the Federal Land Policy and Management Act of 1976, if and when no further military need for property exists, then the land can be transferred between agencies.

For a tribe to recover land, this means that the land is first transferred from the Department of Defense to the Secretary of Interior. The secretary, in turn, has to agree that the lands are suitable for public domain.

However, historically, "the transfer of administrative control from one federal agency to another is categorically excluded from environmental review due to the fact that this type of action normally does not have an effect on an individual or the environment."[109] This loophole means that if and when we get land back, it may very well be contaminated with whatever the military left behind.

> [Unexploded] ordnances on formerly used defense installations probably contaminates 20 to 25 million acres in the United States, and the number could be as high as 50 million acres. Sadly, no one can give us an accurate appraisal of the problem. What we do know is at the current rate of spending, it will take centuries, maybe even a thousand years or more, to return this land to safe and productive use. Some may be so damaged, we may not attempt to clean it up.[110]

> DoD's clean-up programs embrace a relative framework … and often do not consider tribal-unique factors such as subsistence consumption, ceremonial use of certain plants and animals, and the low population densities that exist on many reservations. As a consequence, DoD sites on Indian lands often receive low relative-risk scores, which means that clean up at these sites may be deferred for many years.[111]

That's unfortunate, particularly if you live there.

THREE CASES OF LAND JURISDICTION TRANSFERS:
NAVAJO, OGLALA SIOUX AND HO-CHUNK NATIONS

The toxicity of military lands has increasingly come into question, and the liability associated with these lands has resulted in some changes in policy. Cases of land jurisdiction transfers include: Fort Wingate on the Navajo reservation, Badger Munitions on the Ho-Chunk reservation and the Badlands Bombing Range on the Pine Ridge reservation. All three sites are in the process of "remediation" by the military or by the tribal community that must live with the damage.

THE NAVAJO NATION AND FORT WINGATE

Fort Wingate is located near Bear Springs and Horse Fenced in Canyon in the territory of the Diné and Zuni people on about 21,000 acres of land. There are, according to reports, thousands of archaeological sites on this former military base.

The lands here had been occupied for thousands of years before the coming of the European colonizers, then the Americans, and with them the US Army.

The more recent history of Fort Wingate is associated with the military seizure of the land in 1850 from Indigenous peoples, the use of it as an interim prison camp and then, for almost 40 years, as a highly toxic military base.[112]

Under the command of the infamous General James Carleton and his loathsome subordinate, Colonel Kit Carson, Fort Wingate became an interim prison camp when Carson's troops forced the Diné people on several death marches, known collectively as the Long Navajo Walk. The army shot stragglers, and many died along the way.

Eighty years later, Fort Wingate became an important location for the testing of Pershing missiles and a storage facility prior to the shipping overseas of many of the weapons used in World War II, resulting in a wide array of toxic impacts.

The Navajo Shush Bi Toh Task Force worked for the return of aboriginal Navajo lands in the closed Fort Wingate Army Depot in the 1990s, although when the group leader Karl Katenay died, so did the task force.[113]

Work continues, however, by the Navajo Nation, and researchers continue to assess the environmental health of the area.

The problems of Fort Wingate mirror those of other former military sites in terms of their toxicity. In the remediation and land discussion between the Department of Interior and the Navajo Nation, different categories of land are identified according to their toxicity.

The Community Environmental Response Facilitation Act (CERFA) was passed by Congress in 1992. Until recently, military lands were covered under CERFA.

These include several categories of CERFA parcels: (1) those that are thought to have been fully remediated; (2) CERFA-qualified parcels with no evidence of storage of hazardous materials for the past year (but may contain radio nuclides, or unexploded ordnance); and (3) disqualified parcels that are heavily contaminated.

Around three-quarters of Fort Wingate is considered qualified to be transferred back to the Navajo Nation, but some 4,533 acres are too toxic to be returned. In all cases, however, groundwater contamination remains a problem.

The Navajo Nation began the process of recovering Fort Wingate from the military in 1993 and has been working on the remediation of this site ever since. Their hope is to return the land for residential use by the Navajo people.

> Fort Wingate Army Depot Activity Area (FWDA) demilitarized and test fired munitions from 1949 to 1993. Many improper waste handling practices such as the pumping of wash water containing explosive compounds which was pumped into storage and drying tanks, and allowed to overflow from tanks was drained onto leaching beds, thereby rendering the depot area and adjacent Navajo owned lands contaminated.

> There are several chemicals that are not mentioned, in the characterization of contaminants present in soils, surface or groundwater that may have been test fired or stored at FWDA such as: white phosphorous, mustard gas, nerve gas, Agent Orange, napalm and biological weapons. Further investigation of soil, ground and surface waters for chemicals commonly associated with periods of

war and the manufacturing of ammunitions is of utmost importance to the impending decisions regarding remediation as well as
to the health and welfare of the future residents of FWDA.[114]

Fort Wingate cleanup and remediation is estimated to require 60–100 years
before the area is rendered safe.[115]

Until about 2005, Wingate Elementary School, a K-8 federally-
funded boarding school for Indian children, was nestled among
abandoned military buildings. Fences and barbed wire encircled
some of the buildings to keep trespassers (and students) out. I
taught middle school science there in 2001. Between the building in which I taught, and the Middle School office building was
a boarded-up structure. It was off limits to anyone at the school,
and presumably belonged to the US military.

One morning, that structure caught fire. Brown smoke billowed
from the windows of the shed, followed by smoke of varying
colors. As I recall, no one on campus (including the Principal)
knew what was stored there. The local fire department was called
in, and school administrators frantically called to federal offices
in Albuquerque and Washington D.C. Within a few hours federal
officials arrived to survey the scene. It was just another reminder
that we were teaching children on militarized land.[116]

THE GREAT LAKOTA NATION AND THE BADLANDS BOMBING RANGE

It is said that if the Great Sioux Nation were in control of its 1851 treaty area, it
would be the third greatest nuclear weapons power on the face of the Earth.

This is due to the vast number of US Air Force, NORAD and other bases
in the Lakota territories now called Nebraska, North and South Dakota,
Wyoming and Montana. Of particular concern to the Lakota Nation, however, is the gunnery range on the Pine Ridge reservation, which is part of a
more recent seizure of land. "[T]he US Government seized 342,000 acres
of the Pine Ridge reservation in South Dakota for a bombing range to train
WW II pilots. The land seizure forced 15 Oglala Sioux families to sell their
farms and ranches for three cents an acre."[117]

The gunnery range, or Badlands Bombing Range, continues to be a source of concern for the Oglala Sioux Tribe, as both live and spent ordnance are found throughout the area.

In the summer of 2004, a "small bomb" was found and detonated in the Stronghold segment of the Badlands Bombing Range. The bomb was an M70, measuring 51 inches long, but was found to be largely innocuous—full of "photo flash powder." The bomb was likely 40 years old, a remnant of the military's use of the land for aerial gunnery and bombing practice. It is not known how many bombs remain in the area.[118]

The Oglala Sioux Tribe is working on the cleanup of the Badlands Bombing Range, under an agreement with the military. The tribe determined that they wished to undertake this responsibility, stating:

> The people of the Oglala Sioux tribe (1) are the rightful owners of the land (2) the bombing range land contains many historic and religious sites (3) the people agreed that they did not want outsiders digging up or removing cultural artifacts belonging to the tribe, selling and making profit from them.[119]

Tribal members were trained by the DOD for ordnance remediation, but upon completion of the training, the funding was no longer available to continue the cleanup.[120]

THE HO-CHUNK NATION AND BADGER MUNITIONS

The Badger Army Ammunitions Plant near Baraboo, Wisconsin, was established by the military in 1942 as a class II military propellant manufacturing installation. The plant produced propellants for small arms, rockets and a host of larger weapons.

Ammunition production ceased in 1975, but the plant occupied 7,400 acres of land, some of which became contaminated with a host of toxic chemicals including chloroform, carbon tetrachloride, trichloroethene and dinitrotoluene. Cleanup costs associated with the plant are upwards of $80 million. The plant now ranks as the 23rd most expensive cleanup project on the Pentagon's list, yet money for such mitigation trickles in slowly.[121]

Over the past two decades, the Ho-Chunk Nation has been seeking return of the lands associated with the former Badger facility, with a focus on

1,520 acres of land considered the least contaminated. An attorney for the
Ho-Chunk working on the case, Samantha Green Deer, reports that the tribe
is cautious and awaiting more "remediation" of the toxic site as required
under the law. The remediation is expensive, and the tribe would prefer that
the military, which made the mess, clean it up.[122]

Interestingly enough—and largely based on the expense of cleanup, it
would appear—new regulations for transfer of military bases to tribal communities have come into effect in the past few years, pushing for a transfer
into fee status as the BIA may be concerned about the liability of the former
defense sites. In each case, an environmental assessment must be done for
each parcel under consideration for return.

With this land the Ho-Chunk plan to create an organic bison operation to
feed the tribal population. The land is currently toxic and the BIA oversees
the transfer to ensure cleanup is performed by the military prior to transfer.
The military is only required, at this time, to clean up the site to minimal
standards. In doing this, the military cleans up the site, but does not remove
intact dangers like asbestos—the military will not remove it unless it is
exposed and poses a health threat.[123]

THE PRICE TAG OF THE US MILITARY'S ENVIRONMENTAL IMPACT
Blowing things up is the military's strong suit, not cleaning up after itself. Of
the whopping federal defense budget of $664 billion (2010) only a tiny fraction
will be spent on cleanup and resolving its impacts on the environment either
locally or globally.

An Associated Press story from 2004 read, "removing unexploded munitions
and hazardous waste found so far on 15 million acres of shutdown US military
ranges could take more than 300 years, according to Congressional auditors."[124]

This cost is now estimated at $35 billion and climbing rapidly. In one report,
the military identifies some 17,482 potentially contaminated sites at 1,855
installations.[125]

The military cleanup budget is not a reflection of the military's environmental impact. And, in reality, rather than clean up the toxins placed in the
environment by the military, the Department of Defense has successfully
limited all liability for much of their own contamination.

THE RANGE READINESS PRESERVATION INITIATIVE

In 2004, the Department of Defense (DOD) introduced federal legislation proposing exemptions from the Resource Conservation and Recovery Act, the Comprehensive Environmental Response, Compensation and Liability Act, and the Clean Air Act.

This proposal was the last of a three-part legislative package called the Readiness and Range Preservation Initiative, through which DOD sought exemptions from several federal environmental statutes in order to ensure military readiness in the face of environmental compliance requirements.

While Congress granted earlier exemptions from the Migratory Bird Treaty Act, the Marine Mammal Protection Act, and the Endangered Species Act, it declined to grant exemptions from the hazardous waste and clean air laws in 2004, though DOD will propose these exemptions again in 2005.

Public interest groups, representatives from local and state governments, scientists and community advocates raised several concerns regarding the proposed hazardous waste law exemptions, most notably that these exemptions were dangerous to the public health, redundant and founded in exaggerated concerns.

Arguably, the current statutory scheme provides DOD with sufficient flexibility to avoid liability while still ensuring unyielding protection for the environment and public health. If the exemptions were to be granted, DOD would not face liability or mitigation responsibility for munitions-based toxic contamination until there was an 'imminent and substantial endangerment' to the public health; at that point, mitigating the hazardous waste and protecting the public health would present tremendous and possibly insurmountable challenges."[126]

–From *Exempting Department of Defense from Federal Hazardous Waste Laws: Resource Contamination as "Range Preservation?"* by Caitlin Sislin, updated in email by Caitlin Sislin and Kahea Pacheco, June 22, 2011

The Department of Defense continued to seek these exemptions over the past few years, but has been unable to secure additional environmental exemptions as of yet.

In particular, in the National Defense Authorization Act for Fiscal Years 2006, 2007 and 2008, the DOD included several key provisions which sought congressional approval to:

- Allow DOD and states up to three years from the start of new military readiness activities to satisfy CAA State Implementation Plan (SIP) general conformity requirements when existing units are relocated or new units are moved to an installation.
- Codify the premise that the use of military munitions on operational ranges does not constitute the generation of solid or hazardous wastes as defined under RCRA.
- Codify the premise that the use of military munitions on operational ranges does not constitute a release as defined under CERCLA, provided that the munitions remain on the range where used and there is no migration of munitions constituents from an operational range to off-range areas.[127]

With these provisions, the DOD has essentially asked Congress to postpone DOD's obligation to conform military readiness activities to CAA requirements and provide exemptions to RCRA/CERCLA's options for litigation concerning the policy to not classify munitions used for military testing and training as a waste management activity or trigger for cleanup requirements. Congress has declined to include any of these provisions in the final bill for those years.

Indeed, in a March 2008 report to congressional committees, the Government Accountability Office (GAO) stated that,

> On the basis of information obtained from the military services on the reliability of their unit readiness data, our discussions with DOD, military services, and NGO officials, and our review and analysis of documents and reports describing the effects of environmental requirements and statutory exemptions on training activities, military readiness, and the environment. . . . DOD has not presented a sound business case demonstrating the need for the proposed exemptions from the Clean Air Act, RCRA, and CERCLA to help achieve its training and readiness requirements.[128]

SAVING LIZARDS FROM THE FERAL CATS OF SAN NICOLAS ISLAND

Hundreds of Native American burial sites, middens and other sacred sites cover San Nicolas, a navy-owned 33-square mile island gunnery range off the coast of Southern California that became overrun with feral cats. They were feasting on cormorants and threatened species of foxes and lizards, so six agencies combined forces and spent $3 million to catch and remove the cats for adoption, using humanely padded traps. Now, comes what may be a larger problem for ecosystem protection: the fact that the US Navy continues to bomb and conduct maneuvers on the ecologically and culturally sensitive area.

GREEN MILITARIZATION: US ARMY BARGES OVER CELILO FALLS

Celilo Falls illustrates the impact of the US military on Indian Country in an entirely different way, at a place on the Columbia River known variously by the indigenous people as *Wyam, N'ch-iwana, Celilo*, where the army decided to repurpose the river to generate the electricity they would need at Hanford and other military-industrial facilities. Being engineers, the US Army Corps of Engineers also wanted to engineer a way to move barges past the portage at Celilo Falls.

The US military first arrived at Celilo Falls in 1805, an expedition led by Lewis and Clark sent into unknown territory to find a hoped-for Northwest Passage, and to claim ownership of everything they liked as "discoverers." At Celilo, they found large villages lining both banks of the river, the epicenter of a vast, salmon-based trading economy that had existed since time immemorial. The people were wealthy, living in harmony with the Creator's gifts, and they greeted the newcomers with generosity and salmon, a food source new to Lewis and Clark.

Only 50 years later, the US Army, supported by white vigilante mobs and aided by repeated outbreaks of new epidemic diseases that decimated the tribes, forced the survivors to sign egregious treaties ceding most of what Congress now called the Oregon Territory, or face extinction.

The Columbia River Treaty tribes—the Yakama, Nez Perce,
Umatilla and Warm Springs Confederated Tribes—were removed
to reservations far from the Columbia River, their village sites
taken over by white "settlers," but the Wyam people remained at
Celilo Village, where they remain today, the oldest continuously
inhabited settlement in North America, dating back more than
12,000 years.

The 1855–56 treaties guaranteed the Columbia River tribes the
right to "take fish at the usual and accustomed places," but the
tribes in the Pacific Northwest at that time were unaware that the
United States had such a bad habit of failing to keep its promises.
The Corps of Engineers has a trust responsibility to uphold the
provisions of those (Columbia River) treaties and those rights.[129]

However, in 1957, the Corps of Engineers ordered the gates shut
at the new dam at The Dalles, and just six hours later the ancient
fishing grounds were inundated and the completely self-sustain-
ing economy destroyed.

Where the fish numbered in the millions, the dams at Bonneville
and The Dalles have rendered every fish run through Celilo
extinct, endangered or threatened. The dollars spent to recover
salmon species now numbers in the billions, and the cost to the
public to maintain the occasional barge passage over Celilo Falls
is beyond calculation.

Hydropower, as tribes have come to know, can devastate vast
areas of Indian Country, covering burial grounds and sacred

*In 1945, US Army General Jonathan
Wainwright requested a tour of Celilo
Falls and a meeting with the Indians who
fished there. Here, he poses with Charley
Quetukhin, left, Wyam Chief Tommy
Thompson, with whom he is shaking hands,
and Thompson's son Henry. Twelve years
later, Chief Tommy Thompson and the Wyam
people witnessed the unthinkable. Photo
courtesy of HistoricPhotoArchive.net.*

sites, killing off fish and other species wholesale, and destroying economies developed over thousands of years. Currently, the Winnemem Wintu in Northern California face yet another round of threats to their homelands with an initiative that would raise Shasta dam and flood still more of their ancient sites.

Hydropower may be green, but it is a mistake to assume that it is cheap.

WHY ARE ALL THOSE RESERVATIONS CALLED FORT?

There are at least 20 American Indian reservations and 17 Canadian Native reserves called Fort something or other. What does this do to our collective psyches as Native peoples—living at or on the Forts? Is this a source of pride, or a reminder of domination? Or is it both?

Names and naming are of great importance and significance to Native peoples. Here's a synopsis of the history of the reservations named Fort:

FORT APACHE

The Fort Apache Indian Reservation is home to the White Mountain Apache. When the army first entered the area, they found the White Mountain Apache living peacefully on their own lands, growing corn as they had for thousands of years. The army nonetheless determined to build a fort to control them and make the Apache dependent on the army for their subsistence. Fort Apache was the last operating cavalry outpost in the United States when the army disbanded it in 1922. The BIA established a boarding school there in 1923 to torment "the Indian" out of Indian children.

FORT BELKNAP

The Fort Belknap Indian Reservation is home to the Assiniboine and Gros Ventre people. It was established in 1888 and named after William W. Belknap, the Secretary of War (1869–1876).

FORT BERTHOLD

Home to the Mandan, Hidatsa and Arikara peoples, the Fort Berthold Indian Reservation was established by the Fort Laramie Treaty of 1851. The reservation bears the name of fur trader Bartholomew Berthold. Created in 1870, the reservation is a pittance of the treaty-guaranteed lands and was later diminished for the Garrison Dam, flooding a quarter of the reservation.

FORT BIDWELL

The Fort Bidwell Indian Reservation, established in 1879, is located in California. The reservation is named after Major John Bidwell. Fort Bidwell was constructed in order to protect settlers from Native people who lived there. The fort was used as a base from which the Modoc War (1872), Bannock and Nez Perce campaigns were waged. The reservation was originally established to control the Paiutes.

FORT HALL

The Fort Hall Indian Reservation was established by the Fort Bridger Treaty of 1868 in the wake of the Bear River Massacre of 1863, in which the US Army killed more than 400 Shoshone men, women and children, as a 1.8 million acre homeland for four distinct bands of Shoshone and Bannock and one northern Paiute band. Located in Idaho, it originated from a trading post near the Oregon Trail and California Trail operated by opportunistic Nathaniel Wyeth, a fur trader.

FORT INDEPENDENCE

Fort Independence Indian Community of Paiute Indians of the Fort Independence Reservation is located in California and was established in 1862 during the Owens Valley Indian War, and reoccupied by the Nevada Volunteers who battled the Paiute in March of 1865 . The reservation was formally established in 1915.

FORT MCDERMITT

The Fort McDermitt Paiute and Shoshone Tribe was established in 1865 and is located in Nevada. It was first called the Quinn River Camp #33 and was then renamed in honor of military District Commander Lt. Col. Charles McDermitt. The fort was created in order to protect the Virginia City-Quinn River Valley-Oregon Road. From this fort, troops were sent to fight in the Snake War, Bannock War and Modoc War and the fort was the longest active army fort in Nevada. In 1889 it was converted to a reservation school.

FORT MCDOWELL

All Apache (Yavapai also) . . . large enough to bear arms who may be encountered in Arizona will be slain whenever met unless they give themselves up as prisoners.

— US Army Dispatch 1864

General Crook and other military officials moved between Fort Whipple, Camp Verde and Camp Grant to destroy the Yavapai and other Native nations of Arizona. The military campaigns continued, with both sides fighting furiously for their territory.

In April 1873, many Yavapai surrendered at Camp Verde, where a reservation was formed. The irrigation systems allowed the reservation to be relatively self-sufficient, but contractors who sought to make money from supplying the government with rations petitioned to have the reservation revoked.

In March of 1875, the Yavapai were forcibly marched 180 miles to the San Carlos reservation, on a winter trek in which 100 perished. The Fort McDowell Yavapai Nation was created in 1903. It was formerly called the Fort McDowell Mohave-Apache Community of the Fort McDowell Indian Reservation. It is named Fort McDowell because the Yavapai Nation was granted 24,680 acres of the old Fort McDowell Military Reserve.

FORT MOJAVE

Originally established as Fort Colorado in 1859, stations were posted along the Colorado River near the head of the Mojave Valley. This provided the base of operations against the Mojave Indians. Abandoned under the order of Brigadier General Edwin Sumner, the War Department eventually turned over the buildings for the establishment of the Indian Service. The Fort Mojave Tribe reservation was established in 1857. It is located in California, Arizona and Nevada. Fort Mojave was used in World War II as a training site for river crossings and other military exercises.

FORT PECK

The Fort Peck Indian Reservation was established in 1871 to exercise control over the Assiniboine and Sioux Indians. The reservation was created from the aftermath of wars such as the Battle of Greasy Grass (the Little Bighorn) in 1876.

The Assiniboine and the Sioux Indians were relocated and forced to go to the Fort Peck Indian Agency and a sub-agency at Fort Belknap. The agency was named after the fur traders Durfee and Peck. The white hunters were merciless in harassing the Assiniboine Indians, such as the horrific event in Cypress Hills that destroyed 40 homes.

FORT PIERCE

Fort Pierce was named after an earlier fort that was constructed in the early 1800s during the period of the Second Seminole War led by Lt. Col. Benjamin Pierce. The fort was created to be the focal supply depot for the army in the Second Seminole War. Today the fort is a park built on Indian burial mounds in Florida.

FORT SILL

Fort Sill was initially staked out in 1869 by Major General Philip Sheridan, commander of the Armies of the West, as an essential strategic base for his campaigns against Native people, men, women and children alike. Troops stationed at Fort Sill included the infamous Seventh Cavalry and a number of black "Buffalo Soldiers."

Sheridan later named the post in honor of his West Point classmate Brigadier General Joshua Sill. The first Indian agent at the post was Colonel Albert Boone, grandson of Daniel Boone.

The Fort Sill Military Reservation was formed from the Apache, Comanche and Kiowa lands by a presidential executive order of March 2, 1892. The Chiricahuas were forced again to move by the US Army and most went to New Mexico while the others stayed on Oklahoma allotments.

There are two cemeteries at Fort Sill, one for army scouts and one for military prisoners—mostly Apaches. Some 78 Apache men and families lived out most of their lives in incarceration at Fort Sill.

FORT THOMPSON

Fort Thompson was established to incarcerate the Dakota after the 1862 Dakota uprising. Many Santee were incarcerated there and many died of starvation and the inhumane conditions at the fort. Later, Fort Thompson became the headquarters for the Lower Yanktonai Sioux and the adjacent Crow Creek and Lower Brule reservations.

FORT YATES

The initial army post was established here in 1863 as the Standing Rock Containment for the purpose of controlling the Hunkpapa, Inhunktowan and Cutheads of the Yanktonais and the Lakota Oyate. Its name was changed by the US Army in 1878 to honor Captain George Yates who was killed at the Battle of the Little Bighorn. Fort Yates was also the headquarters of the US Standing Rock Indian Agency.

After out-maneuvering the US military in many battles, including the Battle of Greasy Grass, Sitting Bull went to Canada. Sitting Bull was initially incarcerated at Fort Randall for two years with a number of his people. He was later imprisoned at Fort Yates, where he was assassinated by Lakota policemen sent by Agent McGlaughlin on December 15, 1890, shortly before the Wounded Knee Massacre took place.

FORT YUMA

Fort Yuma was established in 1850 in order to control the Yuma Indians that were located near the Colorado River and to guard the emigrant passage to California. The fort was turned over to the Yuma Indian Reservation in 1892.

KIT CARSON, FORT CARSON
AND THE WARS IN IRAQ AND AFGHANISTAN

In 2003, then-Secretary of Defense Donald Rumsfeld lionized Kit Carson, the "Indian-killer" and extended his notoriety to the US war in Iraq:

> In the global war on terror, US forces, including thousands from this base, have lived up to the legend of Kit Carson," Rumsfeld said, "fighting terrorists in the mountains of Afghanistan, hunting the remnants of the deadly regime in Iraq, working with local populations to help secure victory. [130]

The above photo was released by Department of Defense Secretary Donald Rumsfeld at Fort Carson. Carefully positioned in the photo are cavalry troops still dressed for the Indian Wars. He's telling the troops they are headed for Indian Country....

The "legend" of Kit Carson is one thing, but the facts of murdering, genocidal, ethnic-cleanser Kit Carson are far different. Let us hope that we are NOT sending troops to murder unarmed civilians, the elderly and the infants, like in the good old days of legendary Kit Carson.

A great deal of the American West is named after Kit Carson. A particularly ironic example is Carson National Forest, named despite his negative ecological impact on the natural world.

Professor Glenn Morris, at the University of Colorado in Denver, details some of Carson's actions that contributed to the mythology of Carson the Indian Killer remaining in present military ideology:

In the bitter winter cold of 1864 (the same winter that hosted the Sand Creek massacre of 300 Cheyenne and Arapaho children, elders, and women less than 100 miles from the current Fort Carson), Kit Carson destroyed the prized peach orchards of the Diné, cutting down over 5,000 trees, with the sole purpose of starving the Diné, and this meant all the Diné—men, women, children, elderly, and sick—into surrender.

Even with this hardship, the Diné resistance continued until the fall of 1866. Carson's most notorious act, however, was the forced march of the Diné over 300 miles across New Mexico to the concentration camp at Bosque Redondo.

Over 300 Diné died from exhaustion, illness or exposure on the forced march—and they may have been the fortunate ones. Once at Bosque, which Hitler later used as a model for his own extermination camps, and which is easily recognizable as the tactical and cultural precursor to Camp X-Ray at Guantanamo Bay and Abu Ghraib prison today, the Diné lived a desperate existence, where hundreds more died of starvation, exposure and disease.

All as a result of the actions of Kit Carson.[131]

Bosque Redondo Concentration Camp, New Mexico Territory, 1864—the reality of Kit Carson's heroism. Courtesy of the State Records Center and Archives. Frank McNitt Papers, Serial #5514; photo #5702. "Navajos under guard at Fort Sumner," ca. 1864. US Army Signal Corps Photo in the National Archives.

IV.

The Military
and the Future

The Bears were different. In times past, they were warriors, the
ogichidaag, those who defended the people. Sometimes they
still are. We are what we are intended to be when we have those
three things that guide our direction- our name, our clan and our
religion.

—Winona LaDuke, Last Standing Woman[132]

So here we are in the seventh generation and well into a new millennium.
We face immense challenges ecologically, economically, socially and indi-
vidually, challenges that threaten humankind and the planet inseparably.

Many of these challenges stem from the historic role of the US military
in implementing the Doctrine of Manifest Destiny. Indeed, creating and
maintaining the worldwide American empire with the most expensive
military on the planet has huge implications—whether in Native America,
Southeast Asia, the Middle East or anywhere else. The costs in every sense
are astronomical.

We face challenges of exceptional severity in human and economic costs
due to the still-unfolding catastrophic decision by the Bush-Cheney administration to invade Iraq and hope like crazy to find some weapons of mass
destruction hidden over there somewhere so they wouldn't look so stupid.
The reality is that weapons of mass destruction remain all over Indian
Country—from Umatilla to the Skull Valley Goshute communities—and the
impacts of the military toxins will likely have major health impacts on these
and other communities.

As well, that the military should label Osama bin Laden, the world's most
despised terrorist, with the name "Geronimo" is an insult to all Native
people. It is also a collective Freudian slip, the Nation's unconscious

thinking spilled out into the open—one of those moments when your "friend" blurts out what he really thinks of you—not so far removed from what General William Tecumseh Sherman had to say about war with the Indians just a few generations ago, as an expression of US military policy:

> But the more we can kill this year, the less will have to be killed the next war. For the more I see of these Indians the more convinced am I that they have all to be killed, or be maintained as a species of pauper.[133]

In short, militarization's historic relationship and baggage, vis a vis indigenous peoples, permeates policy and practice, and although the Indian Wars were technically over by 1900, it seems that they remain—in ongoing pollution, destruction of peoples, land seizures and metaphor.

THE END OF MANIFEST DESTINY ... THE RISE OF PLAN B 4.0

Transforming the role and mission of the US military, the most powerful institution in the nation and in the world, is perhaps the single most important factor in the equation. The challenges we face in the twenty-first century are unlike anything the world has seen before, this time with elevated levels of poisons, toxins, radioactivity and greenhouse gases.

The reality is that we have the financial and technical resources to save Mother Earth, it is just that they are not being brought to bear in the right ways: in the direction of protecting the planet, restoring topsoil, cleaning and preserving aquifers and stopping global climate destabilization. Much of the critical resources and a good portion of the world's most significant technological leaps remain in military hands.

Lester Brown, *in Plan B 4.0*, a publication of the Worldwatch Institute, discusses the financial allocations essential to transforming the world's social and environmental destruction. In simple terms, he says we need a reallocation of resources from the military toward real world security.

In short, Earth restoration efforts are critical to world security. Climate change is viewed as one of the single most destabilizing factors in world economic, political and subsequent military changes; people who are embedded in famines (Somalia), or made refugees by climate change-related disasters (tsunamis) need food and resources and are prey to militarization.

The Worldwatch Institute proposes an allocation of resources for world security. This includes preserving topsoil (with an estimated cost of $24 billion annually), protecting biodiversity ($31 billion annually), renewable energy, access to birth control, and stabilizing water tables—and can be actualized with an appropriation garnered from present world military budgets.

In a streamlined budget, the Worldwatch Institute suggests that $187 billion annually over the next ten years, plus an application of political will and technical support, would be the way to secure our future both ecologically and in terms of human dignity—essential elements of peace. This represents some 13 percent of world military budgets, or one-third of the US military budget.[134]

The ongoing wars in Iraq and Afghanistan are expected to stretch out beyond 20 years with total costs numbering in the trillions of dollars. Much of that expense is allocated to blowing things up, or building or making things that get blown up or abandoned, and all with terrible levels of human suffering and enormous unremediated environmental damage.

The issues of military toxins and military occupation of lands remain human rights and environmental justice issues worldwide. Rather than continue a practice of avoidance and failing to plan to clean up toxic messes, cleanup and prevention should become a meaningful part of military practice.

The Congressional Budget Office recently released its estimate of the total annual costs of the wars in Iraq and Afghanistan, in addition to the funds already spent over the past ten years, projected out to 2021:

> Over the next ten years, CBO projects that war costs for DOD, State, and VA could require an additional $496 billion assuming troop levels fall to 45,000 in 2015 and remain at that level. This estimate is between its previous estimate for a faster drawdown by 2013 and a slower drawdown by 2015.

> If these CBO projections are added to funding already appropriated, the total cost of Iraq, Afghanistan, and enhanced security or other contingency operations could reach $1.8 trillion by FY 2021.[135]

THE MILITARY'S GREEN ECONOMY
POTENTIAL: HOMELAND SECURITY

In 2009, the US Air Force cracked the top-twenty list for renewable energy consumers in the United States, following the cities of San Francisco and Portland, Oregon.

The US military presently derives 9.8 percent of its power from renewable and alternative energy sources, which is higher than the national average.

As one of the largest ticket items in the federal budget, the military occupies a key strategic position in the development of markets for renewable energy and locally produced foods.

Since 2008, the military has increased its efficiency in office buildings and housing and has just received around $400 million from the Obama Administration for new research on renewable energy and to broaden applications of green technologies for their facilities.

Largely under the mandates of reducing costs and securing reliable and local energy sources, the Cannon Air Force Base in New Mexico has been purchasing wind power since 2002. Other bases purchasing wind power include Fairchild Air Force Base in Washington State, which gets nearly 100 percent of its energy from renewable sources, and Ellsworth Air Force Base, which has been buying wind power from the Rosebud Sioux Tribe.

The largest new solar panel installation on an industrial building is a military facility. Of particular note in cost savings and innovation is work underway at Fort Irwin, in the midst of the Mojave Desert. When Brigadier General Dana Pittard assumed command of the fort, he noted that most of the troops were housed in rented tents, using air conditioners powered by diesel generators at an annual cost of around $3 million.

A $22 million investment replacing the tents with insulated semi-permanent tents would save the army around $100 million in the next five years. Reducing generator use on the air conditioners through efficiency will cut carbon emissions by around 35 million pounds a year, the equivalent to taking some 3,500 vehicles off the road.[136]

Another Mojave Desert base, a Naval Air Weapons station at China Lake, is entirely powered by geothermal energy generated below the Earth's surface.

The reality is that both the money and innovation potential in the military dwarfs all other domestic budgets, and this fact creates an enormous opportunity to establish a twenty-first century Marshall Plan for the green economy, as a matter of homeland security.

ON THE FUTURE OF WAR
AND A CLEAR MANDATE TO SUPPORT VETERANS

In terms of the impacts of the military on people, there is no way to avoid PTSD or traumatic brain injuries (TBI) and traumatic amputations. This is the nature of modern asymmetrical warfare, without clear battle lines, where IEDs can detonate anywhere, and in an age where US troops are openly overused, deployed into combat again and again, year after year, like never before in the history of this nation.

There is no way to lessen the horrors of war. There is, however, a clear mandate to support the resources essential for veterans and their mental health, as well as the mental health of their families and their communities, and the mental health of Indian Country.

Unfortunately, that mandate exists in political rhetoric and countless yards of yellow ribbon alone, as the nation chronically fails to budget adequate resources to meet the needs of the wounded veterans that it creates. These facts characterize the entire history of the wars in Afghanistan and Iraq.

In a report titled "The Cost of Iraq, Afghanistan, and Other Global War on Terror Operations Since 9/11" the Congressional Research Service puts the known total costs at $1.21 trillion, of which only 1 percent is designated for veterans' health care.[137]

A CALL FOR A HOLISTIC REPURPOSING OF MILITARY RESOURCES

There is a real opportunity to train veterans to create or to take advantage of opportunities to build a self-reliant, sustainable US economy. In very real terms, the skill sets learned during military service can be reapplied to environmental, renewable energy and food systems work, creating countless opportunities for Native American and other veterans to exercise self-determination at home in their communities.

The military provides some of the best training grounds for the green economy. An engineer trained in the military has skills that transfer to civilian wind or solar installations. The military also possesses some of the most advanced technologies in renewable energy that are not yet available to civilians. For instance, the military is developing some of the best mid-sized wind technology in the world, and this could well be used in Native communities.

Indeed, on the White Earth Reservation we have used this model to adapt the skills of military engineers to help with a civilian installation of a 75-kilowatt Lolland wind turbine. There are new training programs offered to military personnel post-service, and more of those could focus on building these types of skills.

PROBLEM–SOLVING HIGH
POST-MILITARY UNEMPLOYMENT RATES

Military men and women transitioning into civilian life face a host of challenges as they compete with the general population during this period of job scarcity. The unemployment rate for veterans between the ages of 20 and 24, for example, is 25 percent.

Unemployment rates in Indian Country are much higher than in the general population, reflecting long-standing national policy as expressed by General Sherman, and the challenges to finding employment there are correspondingly greater. We are indeed often "paupers" in our own land.

HIRING HEROES, THE UNEMPLOYED
OGICHIDAAG AND JOB CREATION

As of this writing, there are some 873,000 unemployed veterans, many thousands already homeless and many more sliding into homelessness, and nowhere are the unemployment and poverty rates higher than in Indian Country.

Among the several remedies that Congress and President Obama are considering to address the problem in general ways, not in any way targeting Indian Country, is the Hiring Heroes Act of 2011.

This legislation would attempt to reverse rising unemployment among our nation's veterans in three ways: (1) by requiring transition assistance for all service members returning home; (2) by modifying federal hiring practices to encourage the hiring of separating service members; and (3) by encouraging the creation of new job training programs aimed at improving the transition from service member to civilian.[138]

NO CORN, NO PHILOSOPHY

My father would say to me: "Winona, I don't want to hear your philosophy if you can't grow corn."

My father would have advised that we focus investments to train and employ our veterans to work on projects that produce healthy food for local consumption, that create local sources of alternative energy, and that result in cleaner air, water and land for all living things. I think he is right. That is long term security.

Veterans, as well as military personnel transitioning back from the wars or those separating into civilian life, could be assigned to work on these projects on their bases, growing food in community gardens, retrofitting buildings, designing or building wind and solar technology, or environmental cleanup.

These projects could be designed to connect with similar projects in their home communities or on their reservations, easing transition, reducing stress in their readjustment as well as in the system itself.

Addressing the reality of militarization's present impacts remains a very essential survival strategy for Indigenous communities and the veterans community. At the same time, we must demand the implementation of the UN Declaration on the Rights of Indigenous Peoples as reflected, in part, by the military's broad impact on Native peoples worldwide.

In recognition of the impact of the military on Indigenous peoples, the United Nations Declaration on the Rights of Indigenous Peoples, passed by the General Assembly in September 2007, specifically states that:

1) Military activities shall not take place in the lands or territories of indigenous peoples, unless justified by a relevant public interest or otherwise freely agreed with or requested by the indigenous peoples concerned.

2) States shall undertake effective consultations with indigenous peoples concerned, through appropriate procedures and in particular through their representative institutions, prior to using their lands or territories for military activities.[139]

In 2010, President Barack Obama pledged that the United States will sign the declaration. Such endorsement by the United States could signal a new era of military accountability to Native peoples. After all, peace is predicated upon a sense of justice and access to adequate ecological and cultural resources for future generations.

MILITARIZATION AND NATIVE CULTURE

After more than 500 years of Indian Wars, boarding schools and living on reservations named Fort, Native communities might also consider some of the permeation of our own cultural practices by military influence. This is a subject that would require much more deliberation, but in writing this book I was struck by a discussion with a spiritual leader of the Winnemem Wintu of California—Caleen Sisk. Her remarks illuminated some of the discussion of how traditions have arisen, and what has influenced our adaptation.

I go to these ceremonies, these feasts, and sometimes it is a bit awkward. I am a headwoman, a medicine woman of my tribe, but they serve all the men first, even the little boys and then finally they come to me ... this is part of militarization and colonization I think. That is what I would say. It's like why women can't dance or sing. They only cook the food and serve it. That is to say, only young women, virgins and young women dance, until they are older, then they are no longer eligible. That is because we used to have these dance houses that were covered. And then, the soldiers made us take the top off the dance houses, so they could watch us ... they would watch, and they would watch those beautiful young Indian women. A prize to look at or to have that is part of the colonization process ... And, somewhere in this process whether in dances or in leadership, it might be that we are overlooking some very powerful people. If you go back, you had the women who were doctors, medicine people. Since the forts were here, that doesn't happen. Medicine people, political leaders, spiritual leaders, who would just happen to be women.

Is it your tradition to leave the women out? You might be missing something.[140]

IN THIS TIME OF THE SEVENTH FIRE

This book was intended to deepen a discussion on forces that surround us, permeate our cultural practices and determine some of our collective psychology, economic options and ecology of our land. The militarization of Indian Country surrounds us, and when we go off the reservation it controls our economy and worldview.

We are the people who have the opportunity to make a difference. In this book, we've provided some useful information on how and why it is incumbent upon us to look critically at the military—a daunting force in the world, and a daunting force in Native America—and consider our alternatives, consider our relationships and to reconsider how we might change our collective paths and transform the role of the US military on the Land and among the People.

It is vital to understand the differences between the use of the military in wars fought to sustain Empire, to maintain an iron grip on populations, land and resources taken as a continuation of the notion of Manifest Destiny, and the use of the military as Ogichidaag, to protect the People and the Land, to defend Mother Earth from those who would destroy her.

For those of military age, this book might prove useful in helping you plan out your future and that of your family, of your community and your people, for we are all related and it is never too early to consider the roles you might play at different stages of your lives as Ogichidaag.

For the community, it is important to prepare for those who will return to you from military service, to understand fully the scope of the problems that await you, recognizing that more than 20 percent of your veterans will need some form of intensive therapy, perhaps for the rest of their lives, and to meet them and their needs proactively.

For the nation, it is important to develop strategies where military resources are increasingly used for peaceful purposes, perhaps none more crucial as elements of true strategic long-term homeland security than achieving sustainable energy independence and food security, and in removing the toxins that already poison the Land and the People, the water and the air we breathe.

> *Water Spirit feelin'*
> *Springin' 'round my head*
> *Makes me feel glad*
> *That I'm not dead . . .*
> *Witchi-Tai-To. . . .*
>   — Jim Pepper, *Witchi Tai To,* 1971

Learn More about
Military Impacts on Native America

The following resources are recommended if you are interested in learning more about the military's impacts on Native America.

WEBSITES

ALASKA COMMUNITY ACTION ON TOXICS
wman-info.org/thenetwork/profiles/alaskacommunityactionontoxics/
index_html?navBatchStart=30

CERFA INFORMATION
www.globalsecurity.org/military/library/report/enviro/EBSFinalPart2.pdf

DMZ HAWAI'I
www.dmzhawaii.org

GUAM BUILDUP
www.guambuildup.com/

THE IMPOSSIBLE DREAM: A TRIBUTE TO NATIVE AMERICAN VETERANS
wn.com/Impossible_Dream__A_Tribute_to_Native_American_Veterans

THE INDIGENOUS ENVIRONMENTAL NETWORK
www.ienearth.org/pops.html

MILITARY TOXICS PROJECT
www.stopmilitarytoxics.org/about.html

NATIVE AMERICANS IN THE MILITARY: PUBLIC AND INDIAN HOUSING
www.hud.gov/offices/pih/ih/codetalk/onap/veterans.cfm

PASKENTA: NOMLĀQA BŌDA (I AM NOMLAKI)
www.dawsonmediagroup.com/DMG/Documentary_Producers_in_
Portland_Oregon_NOMLAQA.html

THE ROLE OF CEREMONY IN SERVICE AND HEALING
www.acf.hhs.gov/programs/ana/veterans/service.html

VA DIRECT HOME LOANS FOR NATIVE AMERICAN VETERANS LIVING ON TRUST LANDS
www.benefits.va.gov/homeloans/vap26–93–1.asp

VETERANS FOR PEACE
www.veteransforpeace.org/

THE WOUNDED WARRIORS PROJECT: "THE GREATEST CASUALTY IS BEING FORGOTTEN"
www.woundedwarriorproject.org

ZOLTÁN GROSSMAN: WAR AND MILITARY LINKS
academic.evergreen.edu/g/grossmaz/warmilitarylinks.html

BOOKS

Begich, Nick, and Jeane Manning. *Angels Don't Play this Haarp: Advances in Tesla Technology,* Anchorage: Earthpulse Press, 1995.

Carroll, Al. *Medicine Bags and Dog Tags: American Indian Veterans from Colonial Times to the Second Iraq War.* Lincoln: University of Nebraska Press, 2008.

Catalinotto, John, and Sara Flounders, eds. *Metal of Dishonor—Depleted Uranium: How the Pentagon Radiates Soldiers and Civilians with DU Weapons.* New York: International Action Center, 2005.

Holm, Tom. *Strong Hearts, Wounded Souls: Native American Veterans of the Vietnam War.* Austin: University of Texas Press, 1996.

Scahill, Jeremy. *Blackwater: The Rise of the World's Most Powerful Mercenary Army.* New York: Nation Books, 2007.

Silko, Leslie Marmon. *Ceremony.* New York: Viking Penguin, 1977.

Notes

1. Sun Tzu, *The Art of War* (Boston: Shambhala Publications, Inc., 1988).
2. bell hooks, *Teaching to Transgress* (New York: Routledge, 1994).
3. Taiaiake Alfred, *Peace, Power, Righteousness: An Indigenous Manifesto* (Toronto: Oxford University Press Canada, 1999).
4. Akwesasne Notes, *Basic Call To Consciousness* (Summertown, TN: Native Voices, 2005), 80.
5. William B. Kessel and Robert Wooster, *Encyclopedia of Native American Wars and Warfare* (New York: Facts on File, 2005), 209–10.
6. Al Carroll, *Medicine Bags and Dog Tags: American Indian Veterans from Colonial Times to the Second Iraq War* (Lincoln: University of Nebraska Press, 2008), 166.
7. Carroll, *Medicine Bags and Dog Tags*.
8. Bill Donovan, "Former Activist Reflects on Fairchild Takeover," *Navajo Times*, February 24, 2005.
9. Carroll, *Medicine Bags and Dog Tags*, 153.
10. Winona LaDuke, *Recovering the Sacred: The Power of Naming and Claiming* (Cambridge, MA: South End Press, 2005).
11. Carroll, *Medicine Bags and Dog Tags*, 92.
12. Naval History & Heritage Command. http://www.history.navy.mil/faqs/faq61-1.htm.
13. Naval History & Heritage Command. http://www.history.navy.mil/faqs/faq61-1.htm.
14. Naval History & Heritage Command. http://www.history.navy.mil/faqs/faq61-1.htm.
15. Naval History & Heritage Command. http://www.history.navy.mil/faqs/faq61-1.htm.
16. John Whiteclay Chambers, *The Oxford Companion to American Military History* (New York: Oxford University Press, 1999).
17. Carroll, *Medicine Bags and Dog Tags*, 203.
18. Carroll, *Medicine Bags and Dog Tags*, 104.
19. Carroll, *Medicine Bags and Dog Tags*, 116.
20. Carroll, *Medicine Bags and Dog Tags*, 104.
21. Carroll, *Medicine Bags and Dog Tags*, 225.
22. John Adair and Evon Vogt, "Navaho and Zuni Veterans: A Study of Contrasting Modes of Culture Change," *American Anthropologist* 51, no. 4 (December 1949): 548–49.
23. Carroll, *Medicine Bags and Dog Tags*, 117.
24. Felicia Fonseca, "Marines Discharge Navajo Healer," *Albuquerque Tribune Online*, January 26, 2007, http://www.abqtrib.com/news/2007/jan/26/marines-discharge-navajo-healer/.
25. John Adair, "The Navajo and Pueblo Veteran, A Force for Culture Change," *The American Indian* 4 (1947): 5–11.
26. Adair, "The Navajo and Pueblo Veteran," 8–9.
27. Carroll, *Medicine Bags and Dog Tags*, 118.
28. "The Ballad of Ira Hayes," words and music by Peter LaFarge.

29. Lawrence William Gross, "Assisting American Indian Veterans of Iraq and Afghanistan Cope with Posttraumatic Stress Disorder: Lessons from Vietnam Veterans and the Writings of Jim Northrup," *The American Indian Quarterly* 31, no. 3 (2007): 373–409.

30. Jim Northrup, Fond du Lac Follies, *News from Indian Country*, February 2005.

31. Jerome Pigeon, "Indian Warriors: Crazy Horse Rides Again" (term paper, Saginaw Chippewa Tribal College, 2010).

32. Joe Klein, "Military Suicides," *Swampland* (blog), *Time*, March 1, 2010, http://swampland.blogs.time.com/2010/03/01/military-suicides/.

33. Chambers, *The Oxford Companion to American Military History*.

34. National Priorities Project, "Cost of War," http://www.nationalpriorities.org/costofwar_home.

35. Lester R. Brown, *Plan B 4.0: Mobilizing to Save Civilization* (New York: W. W. Norton & Co., 2009), 264.

36. Carroll, *Medicine Bags and Dog Tags*, 204.

37. Thom Shanker, "Bad Economy Drives Down American Arms Sales," *New York Times*, September 12, 2010, http://www.nytimes.com/2010/09/13/world/13weapons.html.

38. Adair and Vogt, "Navaho and Zuni Veterans."

39. Adair and Vogt, "Navaho and Zuni Veterans."

40. Interview with John Redhouse, April 28, 2010.

41. Adair, "The Navajo and Pueblo Veteran," 6.

42. Ruth Roessel and Broderick H. Johnson, *Navajo Livestock Reduction: A National Disgrace* (Tsaile, AZ: Navajo Community College Press, 1974).

43. Judy Pasternak, *Yellow Dirt: An American Story of a Poisoned Land and a People Betrayed* (New York: Simon and Schuster, 2010).

44. Trib Choudhary, "2005–2006 Comprehensive Economic Development Strategy of the Navajo Nation," http://www.navajobusiness.com/pdf/CEDS/CEDS%20 2005%20-%2006%20Final.pdf.

45. Choudhary, "2005–2006 Comprehensive Economic Development Strategy."

46. Choudhary, "2005–2006 Comprehensive Economic Development Strategy."

47. Department of Defense Office of Small Business Programs, "Indian Incentive Program," http://www.acq.osd.mil/osbp/programs/iip/index.htm.

48. Matthew Potter, "US Department of Defense Awards Keres Consulting Contract for Environmental Mitigation Support," *Defense Procurement News*, August 26, 2009.

49. EarthTalk, "What is the US Military doing to reduce its carbon footprint?" *New Hampshire Public Radio*, October 31, 2010, http://www.nhpr.org/what-us-military-doing-reduce-its-carbon-footprint.

50. Chad R. Wilkerson, "The National Defense Boost in Rural America," *Main Street Economist* 3, no.4 (2008), http://www.kansascityfed.org/publicat/mse/MSE_0408.pdf.

51. Interview with Barth Robinson, Radiance Technologies, April 29, 2009, Mission, South Dakota.

52. Staff, "Raytheon's NAPI facility celebrates 20 years," *Indian Country Today*, September 4, 2009, http://www.indiancountrytoday.com/national/56990657.html.

53. Staff, "Raytheon changes New Mexico facility's name to reflect Navajo heritage," *Indian Country Today*, November 24, 2009, http://www.indiancountrytoday.com/archive/72836042.html.

54. United States Senate Committee on Homeland Security and Governmental Affairs Subcommittee on Contracting Oversight, "New Information about Contracting Preferences for Alaska Native Corporations (Part II)," http://mccaskill.senate.gov/files/documents/pdf/071509/ANC.pdf.

55. Stuart Archer Cohen, "Wearing a Blackwater Uniform," *Stuart Archer Cohen*, September 26, 2008, http://stuartarchercohen.com/2008/09/26/wearing-a-blackwater-uniform/.

56. Bill Sizemore, *The Virginian-Pilot,* June 28, 2011.

57. Ibid.

58. Bill Sizemore, *The Virginian-Pilot,* June 9, 2011.

59. Arthur Westing, "Ecological Effects of Military Defoliation on the Forests of South Vietnam," *BioScience* 21, no. 17 (September 1, 1971): 893–98.

60. Vo Quy, "Statement to the House Subcommittee on Asia, the Pacific and Global Environment," June 4, 2009.

61. "Billy Walkabout, Decorated American Indian Veteran, Dies at 57," *USA Today,* March 11, 2007.

62. Autumn Rain Eyes, "Lifesaver Hero: Billy Walkabout," August 18, 2006, http://www.myhero.com/myhero/heroprint.asp?hero=Billy_Walkabout_06_ul.

63. Jim Harding, *Canada's Deadly Secret: Saskatchewan Uranium and the Global Nuclear System* (Winnipeg, Alberta: Fernwood Publishing, 2007).

64. Harding, *Canada's Deadly Secret,* 250–51.

65. DMZ Hawai'i, http://www.dmzhawaii.org/?page_id=1347.

66. Ibid.

67. Rosemarie Bernardo, "Uranium Revelation Upsets Isle Activists," *Honolulu Star Bulletin* 11, no. 6, January 6, 2006.

68. Los Alamos National Laboratory, qtd. in Ward Churchill and Jim Vander Wall, *Agents of Repression: The FBI's Secret Wars against the Black Panther Party and the American Indian Movement* (Cambridge, MA: South End Press, 2002), 134.

69. Harding, qtd. in Ward Churchill, *Struggle for the Land: Native North American Resistance to Genocide, Ecocide, and Colonization* (San Francisco: City Lights Books, 2002), 266.

70. Gregory Hooks and Chad L. Smith, "The Treadmill of Destruction: National Sacrifice Areas and Native Americans," *American Sociological Review* 69, no. 4 (2004): 558–75.

71. Winona LaDuke, *All Our Relations: Native Struggles for Land and Life* (Cambridge, MA: South End Press, 1999).

72. Hooks and Smith, "Treadmill of Destruction," 563.

73. Fine and Remington, qtd. in Hooks and Smith, "Treadmill of Destruction."

74. Fine and Remington, qtd. in Hooks and Smith, "Treadmill of Destruction," 564.

75. Brophy et al, qtd. in "Treadmill of Destruction," 564.

76. Peter Ritter, "Nuke 'Em! Xcel energy spearheads a high-stakes plan to store nuclear waste on a tiny, dirt-poor Indian reservation in the Utah desert," *City Pages,* May 12, 2004, http://www.citypages.com/2004-05-12/news/nuke-em/.

77. "Utah base open after missing nerve agent vial located, officials say," *CNN,* Jan 27, 2011, http://www.cnn.com/2011/US/01/27/utah.base.lockdown.

78. Brenda Norrell, "Skull Valley's Nerve Gas Neighbors," *Indian Country Today,* October 26, 2005, http://www.redorbit.com/news/science/285387/skull_valleys_nerve_gas_neighbors/.

79. Los Alamos Study Group, http://www.lasg.org/technical/plutoniumprimer.htm.

80. US Senator Frank H. Murkowski, speaking at the Workshop on Arctic Contamination, Anchorage, Alaska, May 3, 1993.

81. T. A. Badger, "Villagers Learning a Frightening Secret: Ecology: US reveals that it buried radioactive soil near Alaska town 30 years ago. Residents fear that the atomic testing may have damaged the food chain," *Los Angeles Times,* December 20, 1992.

82. "Cleanup Chronology Report for Fort Greely SMDC Nuclear Reactor SM1A," Contaminated Sites Database, Alaska Department of Environmental Conservation, http://www.dec.state.ak.us/spar/csp/search/IC_Tracking/Site_Report.aspx?Hazard_ID=1706.

83. Pam Miller, "Overview of Military Sites in Alaska Impacts to Environment and Communities," Alaska Community Action on Toxins, http://www.akaction.org/Overview_Military_Sites_in_Alaska_Impacts_to_Environment_and_Communities.htm.

84. Hooks and Smith, "Treadmill of Destruction."

85. LaDuke, *All Our Relations,* Virginia Sanchez interview.

86. LaDuke, *All Our Relations,* Virginia Sanchez interview.

87. Ward Churchill and Sharon Helen Venne, eds., *Islands in Captivity: The International Tribunal on the Rights of Indigenous Hawaiians* (Boston: South End Press, 2004).

88. Interview with Kaho'olawe Commissioner Craig Busby, January 17, 2009.

89. Winona LaDuke, "Homeless in Hawaii: More Land for the Military than for Hawaiians," *Indian Country Today,* August 3, 2004, http://www.envirosagainst-war.org/know/read.php?itemid=6951.

90. Jim Albertini, Nelson Foster, Wally Inlis and Gil Roeder, *The Dark Side of Paradise: Hawaii in a Nuclear World* (Honolulu, HI: Catholic Action of Hawaii/Peace Education Project, 1980), 3.

91. CIA, *The World Factbook,* https://www.cia.gov/library/publications/the-world-factbook/index.html.

92. Ann Scott Tyson, "New US-Japan Plan to Realign Military Defenses," *Washington Post,* October 30, 2005, http://www.washingtonpost.com/wp-dyn/content/article/2005/10/29/AR2005102901207.html.

93. Jared Blumenfeld, EPA Regional Administrator, to Roger M. Natsuhara, Acting Assistant Secretary of the Navy, February 17, 2010, http://yosemite.epa.gov/oeca/webeis.nsf/(PDFView)/20090394/$file/20090394.PDF?OpenElement.

94. Blumenfeld to Natsuhara.

95. Blumenfeld to Natsuhara.

96. Current documents on the Environmental Impact Statement are available at the Guam US Navy Department website: "Guam and CNMI Military Relocation—Environmental Impact Statement," http://www.guambuildupeis.us.

97. Howard P. Willens and Dirk Anthony Ballendorf, *The Secret Guam Study: How President Ford's 1975 Approval of Commonwealth was Blocked by Federal Officials* (Mangilao and Saipan: University of Guam and Micronesian Area Research Center, 2004).

98. "Pagat firing range may be moved to Tinian," http://www.mvariety.com/2010102131321/local-news/pagat-firing-range-may-be-moved-to-tinian.

99. Karen Capuder, "Nisqually Military Research," Evergreen State College (2002).

100. Karen Capuder, "Nisqually Military Research," Evergreen State College (2002).

101. Karen Capuder, "Nisqually Military Research," Evergreen State College (2002).

102. Karen Capuder, "Nisqually Military Research," Evergreen State College (2002).
103. Alan Frazier, Nisqually Tribal Administrator, interviewed by Karen Capuder, 2002.
104. Hooks and Smith, "The Treadmill of Destruction," 564 n1.
105. Lynn Porter, "Introduction to Hanford Issues," January 2004, http://www.hanfordwatch.org/introduction.htm.
106. Confederated Tribes of the Umatilla Indian Reservation, Umatilla Chemical Depot Policy, prepared for the Confederated Tribes of Umatilla Indian Reservation Science and Technology Committee, March 2009.
107. Sara Miller Llana, "US guns fuel Mexico drug war? The politics behind the issue," *Christian Science Monitor,* June 15, 2011.
108. John Dougherty, "One Nation Under Fire," *High Country News,* February 19, 2007, and Evan Perez, "An American Gun in Mexico," *Wall Street Journal,* May 21, 2011.
109. Valerie Rangel, *Base Realignment and Closure (BRAC) Clean-up Plan, Fort Wingate Depot Activity, Gallup, New Mexico.* Draft Version 2. Earth Technology, Alexandria, VA.,1995.
110. Blumenauer, qtd. in Hooks and Smith, "The Treadmill of Destruction," 565.
111. Hooks and Smith, "The Treadmill of Destruction."
112. Elaine W. Higgins and Fort Wingate Centennial Commission, *The Bear Springs Story, 1850 1960: A History of Fort Wingate, McKinley County, New Mexico.* Information was gathered from Ralph Emerson Twitchell, *The Leading Facts of New Mexican History,* vol. 3 (Torch Press, 1917).
113. John Redhouse, personal interview.
114. Rangel, *Base Realignment and Closure (BRAC) Clean-up Plan.*
115. Higgins, *The Bear Springs Story.*
116. Micheal Baumrind, a former teacher at the Wingate Middle School, sent this statement on May 27, 2011.
117. Sam Featherman, qtd. in Hooks and Smith, "The Treadmill of Destruction," 565.
118. LaDuke interview, David Catches Enemy, Natural Resources Director, Oglala Sioux Tribe, April 28, 2010.
119. Rangel, *Base Realignment and Closure (BRAC) Clean-up Plan,* appendix.
120. LaDuke interview, David Catches Enemy, April 28, 2010.
121. Winona LaDuke, Honor the Earth Newsletter Military and Native's Article, Samantha Greendeer.
122. Nellis Kennedy-Howard, personal interview with Samantha Greendeer, 2010.
123. Nellis Kennedy-Howard, personal interview with Samantha Greendeer, 2010.
124. John Heilprin, "300 years for cleanup? " AP Archive, January 17, 2004.
125. National Research Council, *Ranking Hazardous-Waste Sites for Remedial Action* (Washington, DC: National Academy Press, 1994).
126. Caitlin Sislin, "Exempting Department of Defense from federal hazardous waste laws: Resource contamination as 'Range Preservation'?" *Ecology Law Quarterly* 32 (3): 647–82.
127. US Department of Defense, Report to Congress on Sustainable Ranges, July 2007, pgs. 9–10.
128. Government Accountability Office, "Military Training: Compliance with Environmental Laws Affects Some Training Activities, but DOD Has Not Made a Sound Business Case for Additional Environmental Exemptions," 5–9.

129. US Army Corps of Engineers—Portland District website, http://www.nwp.
     usace.army.mil/tribal/home.asp.
130. American Indian Movement of Colorado, "The US Empire—Then and Now,"
     American Indian Movement of Colorado, May 28, 2004.
131. American Indian Movement of Colorado, "The US Empire."
132. Winona LaDuke, *Last Standing Woman* (St. Paul, MN: Voyageur, 1997).
133. General William Tecumseh Sherman's letter to John Sherman, September
     23,1868, The Library of Congress.
134. Brown, *Plan B 4.0,* 263.
135. Congressional Research Service, "The Cost of Iraq, Afghanistan, and Other
     Global War on Terror Operations Since 9/11," March 29, 2011, http://www.fas.
     org/sgp/crs/natsec/RL33110.pdf.
136. Alexandra Zavis, "Military embraces green energy, for national security rea-
     sons," *LA Times,* April 26, 2009.
137. Congressional Research Service, "The Cost of Iraq."
138. Isabel Black, "IAVA Helps Unveil Hiring Heroes Act of 2011," *Iraq and
     Afghanistan Veterans of America,* May 12, 2011, http://iava.org/blog/iava-
     member-veterans-help-announce-critical-jobs-legislation. "The Hiring
     Heroes Act of 2011," http://murray.senate.gov/public/index.cfm?a=Files.
     Serve&File_id=0ea542fe-c8c9-4d9a-ae4d-bc67ffa0f909.
139. UN General Assembly, *United Nations Declaration on the Rights of Indigenous
     Peoples: Resolution,* adopted by the General Assembly, 2 October 2007, A/
     RES/61/295, available at: http://www.unhcr.org/refworld/docid/471355a82.
     html.
140. Caleen Sisk, Winnemem Wintu First Nation, interview by Winona LaDuke at
     the UN Permanent Forum on Indigenous Issues, 2011, New York.